In *Homemade Simple*, veteran cookbook author Amanda Ha[...] shares her joyful cooking manifesto: eat well, connect with loved ones, and integrate healthy, stress-free family meals into your busy life. With more than 100 recipes that maximize flavor in minimal time, Haas provides pantry must-haves, meal-planning ideas, prep and cook times, and tips for transforming recipes into gluten-free, vegetarian, vegan, and dairy-free dishes. Including a foreword by acclaimed cookbook author and television star Ayesha Curry, there is also an entire chapter devoted to staple recipes, such as Change-Your-Life Chicken Stock and Chimichurri, inspiring flexible meals using whatever is on hand. Haas offers delectable recipes for breakfast, snacks, sides, mains, and desserts—such as Veggie Scramble with Goat Cheese, Buffalo Cauliflower Hot Wings, Chicken-Coconut Red Curry Soup, Sheet-Pan Halibut with Pesto and Spring Vegetables, and Pear-Blueberry Crisp—proving that making homemade meals doesn't have to be hard, take a lot of time, or cost a lot of money to be simply delicious.

"Amanda is such a good cook that it hurts my feelings. This is her deal, and you're about to see why. I kid you not, while I was just reading the unpublished manuscript, I put ingredients for five of her recipes in my online grocery cart. I refuse to sacrifice taste or decadence, and Amanda serves up an entire cookbook of bangers. Just buy this cookbook and thank me later."

—**Jen Hatmaker**, *speaker, host of the* For the Love *podcast, and four-time* New York Times–*bestselling author of* Feed These People

"**Amanda's my ultimate kitchen hype woman! The nourishing recipes in her new cookbook,** *Homemade Simple*, **will inspire and empower you to make dynamite home-cooked meals with minimal effort and maximum flavor.**"

—**Michelle Tam**, New York Times–*bestselling cookbook author and creator of* Nom Nom Paleo

"**Amanda's done it again! Simple family classics they'll request on repeat, layered with batch cooking how-tos and realistic weekly meal planning.**"

—**Julie La Barba**, *MD, FAAP; board-certified pediatrician, host of the* Paging Dr. Mom *podcast, and mother of four*

AMANDA HAAS

HOMEMADE SIMPLE

Effortless Dishes for a Busy Life

Foreword by
AYESHA CURRY

Photography by
KATHLEEN SHEFFER

CAMERON + COMPANY
Petaluma, California

TABLE OF CONTENTS

Ya Basic

Basically Breakfast

Simply Snacks

Scrumptious Salads

A Soothing Bowl of Soup

Big, Bold Veggies

It's All About Dinner

Sweets are for Sundays

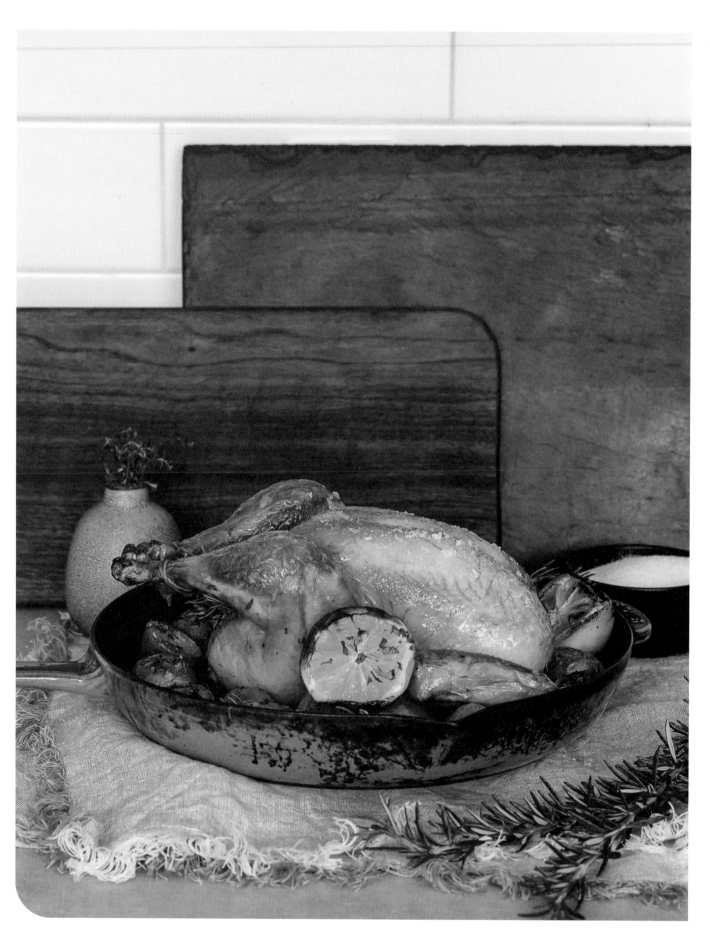

FOREWORD

I t's hard to believe that Amanda and I have been friends for a decade now! When we met, I was a mother of one with big dreams of sharing my cooking with the world. Fast-forward to today, and I am a mother of three with a husband whose career doesn't seem to slow down, and I've created my own space in the food world, which has brought me so much joy!

Amanda and I became friends over our shared passion for cooking, and I believe it's because we share such similar motivations for cooking in the first place. Making a meal for the people I love continues to be one of the most important responsibilities I have in this full life of mine. Whether I'm just home from a work trip or I just want to spend time with my three kids and husband on a Sunday morning, I choose to cook for us. Why? Because cooking doesn't have to be fancy, time consuming, or complicated to accomplish what I'm trying to do: nourish my family while giving us the ultimate gift of being together.

In *Homemade Simple: Effortless Dishes for a Busy Life*, Amanda reminds us why she was meant to write cookbooks. These hundred-plus recipes embody her cooking philosophy, which has developed and solidified over the past thirty years. It starts with her belief that simply getting in the kitchen and making something with your own hands is enough. Her recipes emphasize the use of a few fresh ingredients coupled with simple cooking techniques to bring out the most in the food while keeping us calm, organized, and in charge. In fact, her best recipes are her simplest and the ones you'll come back to again and again.

In this book, Amanda also shares her methods for meal planning and entertaining that make it easy to feed your family and friends amidst the million distractions that take us away from our best intentions to cook at home more. She and I believe that if you "plan your work and work your plan," cooking or entertaining isn't stressful. (Yes, I said that it's not stressful!) Many of her tips and tricks are the reason you'll find me opening my home to loads of family and friends during the busiest times of my life.

I'm so happy Amanda took the time to write these recipes down for all of us. They're the ones you'll turn to time and time again. So, enjoy this book, friends! We can't wait to see what you cook.

—*Ayesha Curry*, NYT *bestselling author, cooking television personality, and entrepreneur*

INTRODUCTION

Hello, friends! It's been four years since I've written a new cookbook. So much has changed for all of us over the past 1,500 days. We've lived through a pandemic—words I never thought I'd say—and world events have taken on a roller-coaster vibe that's not really my style. We've been asked to process so much conflicting information in such a small amount of time, something that I don't think human beings are necessarily equipped to handle. Anthropologists remind us that we used to live in small village settings, and the only "news" we had access to was what was going on in our small worlds. I don't know about you, but having access to an entire world's worth of events in real time has left me feeling overwhelmed and pretty anxious on occasion. So, when we as a country rounded the corner into the second year of the pandemic, I decided to make some changes to my daily routine in order to reduce my stress and get back to the few things that brought me and my family real joy and connection.

My routine shifted drastically as I eliminated a lot of the "should do's" in my life. Instead, I focused on just a few things each day: spending two to three hours working productively; moving my body by walking or dancing; connecting with my sons and my best friend Sunny's family (who happened to live down the street); and cooking for myself and my boys while they sat here for hours and hours every day, attending school from home. I literally let the rest of my priorities fall away.

The things we wound up enjoying the most during our time at home were the simplest pleasures. I'd hop on Instagram Live while I was making lunch for the three of us and interact with my friends. The boys and I ate lunch together; watched *The Office* from start to finish; and walked to town and back, saying hello to all the neighbors who were doing the same. Sometimes the boys would play cornhole out back with Sunny's boys when online school became too rote to bear.

During this period of suspended time in our lives, my sons kept asking me to cook the dishes I had made for them when they were little. As I thumbed through old recipes and unearthed hundreds of them from my first blog *One Family, One Meal*, it was easy to understand why—the recipes were absolutely delicious. But then I noticed that they were also simple to make. I started taking requests, and each time I made an old favorite, I'd look for ways to make them a little more healthful. This usually meant using as many

whole ingredients as possible which led to discovering even easier methods for cooking the recipes that saved me and others time in the kitchen.

As I cranked out simple recipes like Mozzarella Chicken Parm and Tex-Mex Skillet Casserole, my boys and my friends were happier than ever. As it turns out so was I, because through these recipes, my family confirmed my long-held belief that we didn't need fancy, complex recipes to eat well and connect with those we loved. Our best moments around the table happened when we all felt relaxed and dinner was easy. For me, that relaxed feeling should always start in the kitchen.

After settling into this cooking routine for a few months, I was inspired to write another cookbook. Normally it takes me a year to let an idea simmer for a book—pun intended!— but this book came together faster than any of my previous efforts because I was so clear on what I wanted to create. I wanted to share recipes that were simple to make, better than takeout, easy on the wallet, and absolutely delicious. I also wanted to share the tools that have now become so ingrained in my approach to cooking that they will help make putting dinner on the table that much easier for anyone. Things like how to plan out meals for a week, budget, create a shopping list, and even determine the pockets of time throughout the week when the actual cooking can happen (instead of waiting until it's dinnertime and everyone is too hungry to think straight). After spending hundreds of hours working on this cookbook, I can say that this is the book I will turn to forever and ever, whether I'm hosting friends, entertaining younger generations, or simply wanting a delicious weeknight meal for myself that will nourish me and bring me joy.

I am convinced that more than anything else on Earth, human beings crave connection and opportunities to come together with people they love and appreciate to create and cultivate meaningful relationships. Sitting down for a meal together is one of the most enjoyable acts for fulfilling connection. The food—or the act of cooking itself—is simply the excuse we need to make it happen.

May this book be the inspiration you need to help tune out the noise of the world, carve out those special moments each week and come together with the people you love, nourish yourselves, and foster those meaningful relationships. It doesn't have to be hard, take a lot of time, or cost a lot of money to be simply homemade and simply delicious!

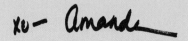

THE HOMEMADE SIMPLE MANIFESTO

Over the many years that I've been cooking seriously, I developed a manifesto of sorts, which is basically my core belief system about what, why, and how I cook. I hope the following declaration will influence your own thinking about cooking as you use this book:

- Cooking can be joyful.

- Good food does not need to cost a lot, take a lot of time to cook, or be difficult to make.

- Anyone can cook!

- Delicious and satisfying recipes can have fewer than ten ingredients.

- You can find everything you need to make simple dishes in nearly any grocery store.

- Using fresh, organic ingredients can improve the flavor of your food.

- Organic produce can make a big difference—see the "Dirty Dozen" (page 25).

- Cooking is an art, which means that you can master techniques and then make them your own.

THE KITCHEN SET-UP

Every time I write a book, I start new lists of what I keep on hand in my refrigerator and pantry, as well as a list of the kitchen tools I currently use most often. For this book, a few ingredients got the boot, simply because I've learned more about how ingredients affect our health. For example, olive oil and avocado oil have replaced other vegetable oils.

Whenever possible, I incorporate almond flour into my baked goods to reduce the amount of refined flour I use. I've also whittled down my choices for gluten-free flours and pastas, choosing those that work best for me and my family.

In terms of cooking equipment, my choices have remained consistent. The pieces I originally invested in, like a high-quality blender, heavy-duty baking sheets, a Dutch oven, and a chef's knife, are still in constant use.

Here's a sneak peek into my kitchen. Use it as a guide to the ingredients and tools you may want to keep on hand to cook basic, healthful food.

Ingredients

By keeping these key ingredients on hand, I'm always able to put together a satisfying meal in no time. Everything on this list can be found in most grocery stores except for my beloved achiote paste for Citrusy Pulled Pork (page 183), which is available in Latino markets and on Amazon. Keep these basics on hand, and you'll have everything you need to get cooking.

PANTRY

I use commonly available and easily stored pantry ingredients to bring out the best flavors in all my favorite dishes. Different vinegars can change up the flavor profile of basic vinaigrettes and sauces, and a spoonful of Dijon mustard can add a little extra punch to almost any sauce. And basic starches and legumes will save the day when you're in a hurry to make dinner.

- Olive oil, extra-virgin and standard
- Avocado oil
- Coconut oil, unrefined (sold in jars and firm until heated)
- Toasted sesame oil
- Vinegars: apple cider, balsamic, red wine, sherry vinegar, white wine vinegar
- Fish sauce
- Canned chipotles in adobo
- Dijon mustard
- Honey
- Maple syrup
- Canned crushed and canned diced organic tomatoes
- Canned black beans, pinto beans, cannellini beans, and garbanzo beans
- Dried black beans and cannellini beans
- French (Le Puy) lentils
- Jasmine rice
- Pasta: fusilli, penne, or spaghetti (regular or gluten-free)
- Coconut milk (regular or light)

PRODUCE

The list of produce you see here contains the ingredients I buy almost every time I go to the market. It's no wonder. All of these fruits and vegetables can be used in a myriad of ways, such as in stir-fries, sauces, egg dishes, juices, and almost any kind of salad. But promise me one thing: Check to see what's in your produce drawer before going to the store. So often leftover produce is hiding there that could be put to good use, such as in soups and egg dishes.

Lemons (Meyer or regular)

Limes

Organic apples (Fujis for snacking)

Green onions

Celery

Carrots

Broccoli and/or cauliflower

Hearty lettuces and organic greens, such as romaine, Little Gem, or kale

Herbs: flat-leaf (Italian) parsley, mint, basil, thyme

Organic strawberries or blueberries for snacking (frozen for cooking)

DAIRY

Cow's milk has gotten a bad rap over the past decade, with many doctors recommending that people with stomach issues, food allergies, and eczema should cut back on it. Some studies show that milk with more A2 protein than A1 protein is more digestible. If you have a problem with digesting milk, look for A2 milk, organic milk from cows that haven't been fed antibiotics, or use lactose-free milk as an alternative. If you prefer, there are several nut and oat milks out there to replace cow's milk in your diet. Do yourself a favor, though, and read the labels first. The fewer ingredients in any processed food, the better.

Organic free-range eggs

Unsalted organic butter, such as Clover or Kerrygold

Grated Parmesan cheese

Milk (preferably A2 or organic oat or nut milk)

SPICES

Spices are flavor bombs that are also loaded with health benefits. They're my secret weapon. The right spice can enhance the simplest of recipes. And because different spices have different health properties, you can increase their benefits by combining them. (Turmeric paired with freshly ground black pepper is the most famous combination. Turmeric is loaded with anti-inflammatory properties, and adding black pepper to it increases its bioavailability by 2,000 percent!) Here are the spices I use most. I also recommend making your own spice blends (see pages 62–64) to use in the recipes in this book and in recipes of your own creation.

Kosher salt, preferably Diamond Crystal Kosher brand

Flaky sea salt, such as Maldon, for finishing

Black peppercorns

Red pepper flakes

Chili powder

Ground cinnamon

Ground cumin

Curry powder

Fennel seeds

Ground ginger

Ground nutmeg

Dried oregano

Ground turmeric

PERISHABLES

Perishables are those foods that are best stored at room temperature. They also happen to be some of the ingredients I rely on the most. I keep onions, shallots, and garlic on a shelf next to my stove top. I store whole pieces of ginger and turmeric at room temp but refrigerate them in a bowl of uncooked rice grains after they've been cut. (It really does help keep them fresh!) Keep potatoes in a cool, dark place such as a pantry, but not in a plastic bag. Sweet potatoes can be stored for a week or more at room temperature in a cool, dry place.

Yellow and red onions

Garlic

Garnet sweet potatoes

Fresh ginger

Shallots

BAKING AND SWEETS

Here's my take on sweets: Instead of trying to develop "healthy" versions of my favorite desserts by substituting ingredients, I follow a traditional recipe and focus on portion control instead. Yes, you can use some almond flour in place of some regular all-purpose flour, and you can substitute coconut sugar in place of brown or cane sugar in some recipes, but my recommendation is to let yourself have the dessert you're craving but stop at one piece! Because I'm gluten intolerant, I've included the best gluten-free flour alternatives for many recipes in this book.

All-purpose flour and Bob's Red Mill Gluten-Free 1-to-1 Baking Flour

Almond flour, preferably Bob's Red Mill (finely ground)

Granulated sugar (it's hard to find fine-grained organic versions, so I often use C&H brand)

Coconut sugar or light brown sugar

Baking soda

Baking powder

Cocoa powder

Pure vanilla extract

NUTS AND SEEDS

Nuts and seeds are the unsung heroes of this book. Nuts are packed with health benefits, including fiber (which most of us need more of), and can help lower bad cholesterol and inflammation in the body. I like to add nuts to food anytime I can to give it crunch, depth, and another layer of flavor. Seeds are also loaded with fiber, healthy fats, and antioxidants, helping to reduce blood sugar, cholesterol, and blood pressure.

> Unsalted roasted organic almonds (slivered and whole)
>
> Unsalted roasted cashews
>
> Walnuts
>
> Pumpkin or sunflower seeds
>
> Pine nuts

FREEZER

I keep frozen ingredients on hand for those days when I have no idea what I'm going to cook. Frozen berries are a perfect go-to for a breakfast smoothie. And I try to keep one or two frozen proteins on hand so I can pull one out in the morning to defrost it by dinner for an easy weeknight meal. Also, I leave plenty of room in my freezer for soups, lasagna, and fruit crisp topping so they're available in a pinch!

> Whole chicken and chicken breasts or thighs
>
> Chicken bones (for stock)
>
> Ground beef (grass-fed) or organic ground turkey
>
> Fish fillets
>
> Mango and açaí berry puree and organic strawberries and/or blueberries for smoothies

The Dirty Dozen & Clean Fifteen

Every year, a nonprofit organization called the Environmental Working Group (EWG) compiles a list of the fruits and vegetables that contain the highest and lowest amounts of pesticides. In 2022, the "Dirty Dozen," which lists produce from the most pesticides used to the least, were listed in the following order (see below). Whenever possible, I try to purchase organic versions of these fruits and veggies to ensure they were not exposed to pesticides. Want to start eating more organic foods but find them to be too pricey? Try buying frozen organics when they're available, including berries and stone fruits.

The EWG also publishes the "The Clean Fifteen," a list of the fruits and vegetables that contain the *fewest* pesticides. You can safely use standard versions of these kinds of produce.

THE DIRTY DOZEN	THE CLEAN FIFTEEN
Strawberries	Avocados
Spinach	Sweet corn
Kale, collard, and mustard greens	Pineapples
Nectarines	Onions
Apples	Papayas
Grapes	Sweet peas (frozen)
Bell peppers and chiles	Asparagus
Cherries	Honeydew melons
Peaches	Kiwis
Pears	Cabbages
Celery	Mushrooms
Tomatoes	Cantaloupes
	Mangoes
	Watermelons
	Sweet potatoes

My Favorite Cooking Tools

GENERAL

Microplane (for grating citrus, garlic, chocolate, ginger, nutmeg)

Tongs! Long ones and short ones (OXO is my favorite brand)

Whisk

Wooden spatula

Wooden spoons

Spoonula (spatula/spoon), large or medium

Fish spatula (my most-used spatula because of its thin, flexible shape)

Dry measuring cups and spoons

Liquid measuring cups (OXO preferred)

Kitchen shears

Set of three stainless steel or glass mixing bowls

Wood carving board

Plastic or fiberglass cutting boards (separate ones for vegetables and fruits vs. chicken and fish)

Bar towels (can be used as hot pads and oven mitts and are easily bleached)

Wire-mesh sieves (small and large)

Colander

Rimmed baking sheets (aka half-sheet pans, to be used for everything!)

Salad spinner

CUTLERY

8-inch (20-cm) chef's knife

7-inch (17-cm) general-purpose knife (Santoku)

9-inch (23-cm) bread knife

Large slicing knife

5-inch (12-cm) utility knife (for fruit, meat, tomatoes, etc.)

4-inch (10-cm) paring knife

COOKWARE/ELECTRICS

Heavy-duty blender

Food processor

Stand mixer

Dutch oven (Le Creuset or Staub)

5-quart (4.7-l) essential pan (a combination sauté pan and skillet)

11-inch (28-cm) nonstick skillet

4-quart (3.8-l) saucepan

3-quart (2.8-l) sauté pan with lid

Charcoal, gas, or pellet grill

MEAL PLANNING: WHY BOTHER?

"I just don't have time to plan!" When I had my first son, I learned the hard way that I didn't have the time **not** to plan. Almost twenty years later, meal planning continues to be my number-one trick for saving time, money, preventing food waste, and reducing the number of my family's last-minute takeout splurges.

I start every week by meal planning. That involves not just cooking ahead, but really strategizing what meals I'll cook when, budgeting and grocery shopping, and transforming leftovers into new dishes. Every Sunday, I fill in the calendar (see page 32) to help me stay organized. You don't need to make twenty-one meals from scratch every week. Instead, pick five or six that you want to focus on and fill the rest in with leftovers, frozen dishes (like THE Lasagna, page 161), and pantry staples (like Better-For-You Granola, page 78).

THE METHOD TO THE MAGIC

- Set a budget.

- Mark the days and meals you want homemade food.

- Mark the days and meals you know you'll be eating takeout, going out to dinner, or be too tired to cook (I never cook on Friday nights).

- Pick an assortment of recipes that work for you.

- Make a note to double up on proteins that could be used to make more than one dish that week.

- Make a shopping list (after checking your pantry, fridge, and freezer to see what you need).

- Master eight to ten recipes to put into weekly rotation.

THE GROCERY PRE-CLEAN

Before I go grocery shopping, I open the fridge and get rid of anything that has gone bad. I consolidate things where possible (more than one container of yogurt, etc.). I wipe down the shelves and make sure nothing is hiding in my produce drawers. I do the same thing with my pantry. Nine times out of ten, I find ingredients I didn't know I had. Then I can make a shopping list without including any foods I already have.

GROCERY PRICES

With the price of food always going up, we are all feeling it at the grocery store. Pay attention to the latest prices of your most-purchased foods so you can judge how much you'll need to spend each time you shop.

THE MAGICAL PREP HOUR

This is the hour I give myself when I come back from the grocery store. I set a timer and see how much food I can prep for the week before refrigerating it. It's so much easier to do the prep ahead of time and store it so it's ready to use! This includes chopping onions, carrots, and/or celery; hard-boiling eggs; washing and drying lettuce; toasting nuts and/or seeds; and roasting chicken breasts to use in different recipes. If I have time, I like to make a vinaigrette or two as well as a sauce that I can use all week long. I often make Balsamic Vinaigrette (page 56) and Chimichurri (page 49) or Classic Basil Pesto (page 51). The vinaigrette lasts all week to use for salads, and the green sauces can be paired with simply cooked chicken or fish or tossed with pasta. I'm always surprised to see how much better I feel about the week ahead after my Magical Prep Hour, because I know that when I'm too tired to cook, I can come up with a homemade meal in a matter of minutes.

And now for the actual cooking!

Homemade Simple Shopping List

PRODUCE

_____
_____
_____
_____
_____
_____

DRY GOODS & CANNED FOODS

_____
_____
_____
_____
_____
_____

MEAT & SEAFOOD

_____
_____
_____
_____
_____
_____

BAKING & SPICES

_____
_____
_____
_____
_____

DAIRY & EGGS

_____
_____
_____
_____
_____

BEVERAGES

_____
_____
_____
_____
_____

FROZEN

_____
_____
_____
_____

OTHER

_____
_____
_____
_____

Making a Weekly Meal Plan

SUNDAY
Breakfast
Lunch
Dinner
Snack

MONDAY
Breakfast
Lunch
Dinner
Snack

TUESDAY
Breakfast
Lunch
Dinner
Snack

WEDNESDAY
Breakfast
Lunch
Dinner
Snack

THURSDAY
Breakfast
Lunch
Dinner
Snack

FRIDAY
Breakfast
Lunch
Dinner
Snack

SATURDAY
Breakfast
Lunch
Dinner
Snack

Three Weeks of My Favorite Meals

A WEEK WITH ENTERTAINING

I love entertaining, but I try to make sure it is as stress-free as possible so I can actually enjoy time with my guests. I like making easy recipes—like the first four in the list below—throughout the week so I have time to prep for weekend entertaining. For example, this week I'm making lasagna for a party on Saturday. The pesto for that will also be used in my egg muffins. I'll prep the lasagna a few days ahead, and I can pop it in the oven while I'm getting the house ready for the party.

Green Eggs and Ham (page 71)

(Actually) Delicious Green Juice (page 80)

The Every-Day Salad (page 106)

Lots-of-Veggie Fried Rice (page 155)

Tofu and Broccoli Stir-Fry (page 154)

Tex-Mex Skillet Casserole (page 175)

Classic Basil Pesto (page 51)

THE Lasagna (page 161)

A WEEK THAT CALLS FOR COMFORT FOOD

Some weeks, I just want comfort food. I make a big batch of Change-Your-Life Chicken Stock (page 43) on Sunday. I then use the stock to make two kinds of soup, and I use the cooked chicken in a soup and a pasta dish.

Chunky Monkey Smoothie (page 82)

Savory Steel-Cut Oats with Greens and Prosciutto (page 73)

Chicken-Coconut Red Curry Soup (page 120)

Hearty Minestrone with Meatballs (page 129)

Creamy Chicken Spaghetti with Lemon and Basil (page 172)

Skillet Chicken with Rosemary and Lemon (page 170)

Warm Brussels Sprouts, Cabbage, and Apple "Slaw" (page 144)

FOR THE OVERLY SCHEDULED WEEK

On those weeks where every minute of every day seems to be scheduled, I choose fast and simple meals like Sheet-Pan Sausage and Polenta with Peppers and Tomatoes (page 178). I make Curry-Lime Vinaigrette (page 57) and Chipotle-Lime Marinade (page 59) at the start of the week to use for multiple dishes. I'll also make a big batch of scones for grab-and-go breakfasts.

EASIER ENTERTAINING

Maybe I just have really cool friends, but I think most people simply like to be invited into their friends' homes to spend time with them. The worst parties are the ones when the host spends all of their time in the kitchen freaking out over details. Even worse, they overcommit to making too many recipes and are literally cooking under pressure while guests are already in their home. My rule is to keep it simple. That means that if I can't make it ahead, I don't make it at all. Exception? Grilling at the last minute, because it's a conversation starter and gets both the cook and the guests outside.

Keep it simple. Choose an entree that can be made ahead, plus a salad and maybe a side dish. Choose one-pot or one-dish recipes, like Citrusy Pulled Pork (page 183), THE Lasagna (page 161), or Sheet-Pan Spiced Chicken Thighs (page 169).

Homemade Simple Party Menus

TACO NIGHT

Shrimp Tacos with Pineapple Salsa (page 156)

Charlie's Guacamole (page 97)

Pickled Onions (page 46)

Vegetarian Black Bean and Chile Chili (page 126)

COCKTAIL PARTY

Flatbread Two Ways (page 93)

Classic Cheese and Charcuterie Board (page 90)

Everything Popcorn (page 95)

Basically Better Spinach and Artichoke Dip (page 91)

GAME NIGHT WITH FRIENDS

Mexican Street Corn-off-the-Cob Dip (page 88)

Chipotle-Lime Wings (page 94)

Everything Popcorn (page 95)

ALL-DAY OPEN HOUSE

Citrusy Pulled Pork (page 183)

Pickled Onions (page 46)

Charlie's Guacamole (page 97)

Citrus–Olive Oil Cake (page 197)

DO-AHEAD DINNER PARTY

Classic Cheese and Charcuterie Board (page 90)

Sheet Pan Halibut with Pesto and Spring Vegetables (page 168)

Italian Orzo Salad (page 115)

Citrus–Olive Oil Cake (page 197)

GIFT-WRAPPING PARTY

THE Lasagna (page 161)

Baby Kale Salad with Delicata Squash and Toasted Walnuts (page 109)

Chocolate-Toffee Crinkle Cookies (page 196)

MOVIE NIGHT ON THE COUCH

Raid-the-Fridge Nachos (page 177)

Everything Popcorn (page 95)

S'mores Bars (page 198)

BRUNCH

Green Eggs and Ham (page 71)

Gluten-Free Lemon-Currant Scones (page 75)

Build-Your-Own Spiced Chia Puddings (page 74)

HOW TO USE THIS BOOK

This book is designed to help you understand each recipe quickly: what's in the ingredient list, how long it will take to prepare, and whether you can do any of it in advance. Here's the key to understanding each recipe visually:

V = VEGETARIAN   DF = DAIRY FREE

VG = VEGAN   Q! = QUICK TO MAKE!

GF = GLUTEN-FREE   MA = MAKE AHEAD

In some recipes you may see *V or *VG and sometimes *GF. This means that there are alternate ingredients listed in the ingredient list that may be used in the recipe to transform it from a non-vegetarian/vegan/gluten-free recipe into one that is vegetarian, vegan, or gluten-free. It's a great way to keep the recipes flexible for anyone's dietary needs!

WHAT DOES "BETTER FOR YOU" MEAN IN THIS BOOK?
Recipes for dishes that are better for you in this book have been tweaked to be more healthful than traditional recipes. For example, they may be lower in fat, sodium, or sugar by using more healthful substitutes for some ingredients, or higher in nutritional value with the addition of vegetables, fruits, nuts, or seeds. But in any case, they will still be satisfying and filled with flavor!

Ya
Basic

CHAPTER ONE

I include a basics chapter in every book I write because after thirty years of cooking, I've mastered a few simple recipes that are the foundation of almost every meal I make. Whether it's an herb sauce that can provide a punch of flavor and a huge dose of health benefits to almost any dish, or homemade chicken stock that can take the simplest soups and braises like Vegetarian Black Bean and Chile Chili (page 126) or Chicken-Coconut Red Curry Soup (page 120) to the next level, these recipes are transformative. I love to come home from the grocery store and make a batch of stock, cooked chicken, a green sauce, and a vinaigrette for the week. Then I know I always have the components available to turn the simplest meals into something great.

Change-Your-Life Chicken Stock

I know it's a tall order to say that homemade chicken stock is going to change your life, but it will certainly make every recipe you make with it taste better! This tends to be the one thing I make every week when I return home from the store. The stock can cook while I unload my groceries and prep a few things for the week. Then I've got shredded chicken to use in all kinds of recipes—like my California Chicken Salad with Peanut Dressing (page 104)—and homemade stock for any soup I feel like making. And if I've got more stock than I need, I freeze it in 4-cup (960-ml) deli containers so it's ready to go whenever I need it.

GF | DF | MA

Prep: 15 minutes

Cook: 2¼ hours

Makes about 4 quarts (3.8 l)

One 4-pound (1.8-kg) chicken, cut into 4 pieces, plus the backbone

1 yellow onion, halved

3 stalks celery, halved crosswise

2 carrots, peeled and halved crosswise

2 cloves garlic, crushed

3-inch (7.5-cm) piece fresh ginger, halved (optional)

Kosher salt

> NOTE: A fat cap will form at the top of stock after it has been refrigerated. To make it more healthful, scrape off that layer before reheating.

In a large stockpot or Dutch oven, combine the chicken pieces, onion, celery, carrots, garlic, and ginger (if using). Add enough cold water to cover the chicken, about 3 quarts (2.8 l).

Place the pot over medium heat and slowly bring to a simmer. As soon as it begins to simmer, use a fine-mesh strainer or sieve to skim off any of the foam (which I affectionately call pond scum) that rises to the surface. Cover partially, reduce the heat to low, and simmer for 45 minutes.

Using tongs, remove the chicken pieces from the pot and discard the vegetables. Let the chicken rest until it has cooled enough to handle, about 10 minutes. Carefully remove the chicken skin and put it back in the pot. Then remove all of the meat from the bones, setting the meat aside and returning the bones to the pot. Shred the chicken, then transfer it to an airtight container and refrigerate for up to 5 days.

Continue to simmer the cooking liquid with the chicken bones and skin for 1 more hour over very low heat, adding more water as needed to ensure the pot is two-thirds full.

Strain the stock through a fine-mesh sieve into a large bowl. It should be fairly bright in color. Stir in 2 teaspoons salt. Taste, adding more salt if necessary. Let cool to room temperature.

To store: Refrigerate in an airtight container or containers for up to 3 days or freeze for up to 1 month.

Eat-Your-Veggies Stock

I make my Change-Your-Life Chicken Stock (page 43) almost every week, as I enjoy the health benefits of bone broth in my diet. However, if you're vegetarian or simply looking to eat a more plant-based diet, this vegetable stock is the perfect foundation. Use it as the base in any of the soups in this book, or even as the broth for Amanda's Mashed Potatoes (page 136). The dried mushrooms add a nice depth of flavor that can easily replace meat-based broths in most recipes.

GF | DF | VG | V | MA

Prep: 10 minutes

Cook: 1½ to 2 hours

Makes about 4 quarts (3.8 l)

3 celery stalks, halved crosswise

3 carrots, roughly chopped

2 yellow onions, halved and skins removed

1 fennel bulb, halved

1 head garlic, halved crosswise

1 ounce (28 g) dried porcini mushrooms

Kosher salt

In a large stockpot or Dutch oven, combine the celery, carrots, onion, fennel, garlic, and dried mushrooms. Add enough cold water to cover the ingredients, about 4 quarts (3.8 l).

Bring to a simmer over medium-high heat, then reduce the heat to low and simmer gently until fragrant and golden brown in color, 1½ to 2 hours.

Strain the stock through a fine-mesh sieve into a large bowl. Stir in 1 tablespoon salt and enough water to equal 4 quarts (3.8 l) of liquid. Taste, adding more salt if necessary. Let cool to room temperature.

To store: Refrigerate in an airtight container or containers for up to 3 days or freeze for up to 1 month.

Parmesan Crisps

These Parmesan crisps check all my boxes for the perfect accompaniment to soup. Make sure to check them after a few minutes to ensure they don't burn and let them cool on the parchment to keep their flat shape.

GF | V | Q!

Prep: 3 minutes

Cook: 4 to 7 minutes

Makes about 12 crisps

1 cup (4 ounces/115 g) freshly grated Parmesan cheese

Freshly ground black pepper

Preheat the oven to 400°F (205°C). Line 2 baking sheets with parchment paper. Spoon heaping tablespoonfuls of the cheese onto the baking sheet, spacing them 2 inches (5 cm) apart. With the back of a spoon, spread each mound into a 2-inch (5-cm) round. Sprinkle each round with pepper. Bake until the crisps are golden, 4 to 7 minutes. Let cool on the baking sheet, then remove with a thin metal spatula. Serve immediately or store in an airtight container for up to 3 days.

Pickled Onions

This is one of my most requested recipes. Once you've tried them, you'll want to put them on everything, including Citrusy Pulled Pork (page 183), Shrimp Tacos with Pineapple Salsa (page 156), and even salads! They're at their best within a day or two but will hold up to 3 days in the fridge.

GF | DF | VG | V | Q! | MA

Prep: 10 minutes, plus 2 hours to pickle

Makes 10 to 14 servings

1 red onion, halved lengthwise and thinly sliced crosswise into half-moons

½ cup (120 ml) fresh lime juice

½ cup (120 ml) fresh orange juice

1 teaspoon kosher salt

1 jalapeño chile, seeded and minced (optional)

In a small, nonreactive bowl, combine all of the ingredients and toss to coat. Cover and marinate in the refrigerator for at least 2 hours before using.

To store: Refrigerate in an airtight container for up to 3 days.

Caramelized Onions

Two words to remember when you're looking for perfectly caramelized onions: low and slow. That's right. Patience is the only thing that will help break down these onions and transform them into the sweet, caramelized, melt-in-your-mouth onions that you'll want to put on everything. If the heat is too high, you'll risk burning them. The same thing will happen if you stop stirring them for too long. So, pour yourself a glass of wine or a delightful fizzy something-or-other and stir until the half-moons are a little scoop of caramelized perfection. Then serve them on top of the Herb-Explosion Burgers (page 189), mixed into roasted vegetables, or on your favorite sandwich.

GF | DF | VG | V | Q! | MA

Prep: 10 minutes

Cook: 30 to 40 minutes

Makes ½ cup (100 g)

2 tablespoons olive oil

2 large yellow onions, halved lengthwise and sliced crosswise into half-moons

Kosher salt (optional)

In a medium skillet, heat the oil over medium-low heat. Add the onions and 1 teaspoon salt. Stir to coat. Cook the onions for 30 to 40 minutes, stirring almost constantly to ensure they don't burn. If the onions start to look burned in areas, reduce the heat to low and add a splash of water to the area that is getting too brown. Use a wood spatula to scrape up the browned bits on the bottom. Once the onions are a deep brown and so sweet you could faint, season with more salt.

To store: Let cool completely and refrigerate in an airtight container for up to 3 days.

Chimichurri (aka Haas Sauce)

When my kids were toddlers, I began making chimichurri to pair with grilled steak and chicken. Because it's loaded with herbs, olive oil, and other raw ingredients that pack a healthful punch, I was thrilled that my kids would literally drink this sauce out of a pitcher if I let them. I've now been making so much of it for so long, everyone started calling it "Haas Sauce." You can see how Grilled Skirt Steak with Chimichurri (page 186) became my most requested recipe from family and friends alike. And because the sauce lasts at least a week in the fridge, it's always available to slather on a sandwich, drizzle onto a breakfast scramble, or eat with a spoon. (Just kidding. Okay, maybe not.) So, after years of slight variations to the recipe, I submit my final—and may I say, best—version yet.

GF | DF | *VG | V | Q! | MA

Prep: 10 minutes

Makes 1¼ cups (300 ml)

¾ cup (180 ml) fresh lime juice (about 1 lime)

1 tablespoon Dijon mustard

3 cloves garlic

2 cups (60 g) fresh flat-leaf parsley leaves, loosely packed

2 cups (60 g) fresh cilantro leaves, loosely packed

¾ cup (180 ml) extra-virgin olive oil

2 tablespoons capers, rinsed

Kosher salt and freshly ground black pepper

1 teaspoon honey or agave nectar (optional)

NOTE: Because the salinity of capers can vary dramatically, I add salt to this sauce at the end.

In a food processor or blender, combine the lime juice, mustard, and garlic. Pulse a few times to break up the garlic. Add the parsley and cilantro and pulse until evenly chopped. Use a rubber spatula to scrape down the sides of the bowl.

Add the olive oil and pulse until a thick sauce forms. For a thinner sauce, stir in 1 or 2 tablespoons of water. Fold in the capers. Taste, adding salt, a few grindings of pepper, and the honey, if desired.

To store: Refrigerate in an airtight container for up to 1 week.

Cheater Romesco

After going steady with chimichurri for a decade, I decided we needed another family sauce. I thought this rich, nutty sauce pureed with roasted red peppers would not be as well received as my green chimichurri, but I was wrong. Now, whenever I'm grilling, I whip up a batch of chimichurri and romesco and offer them both to slather on tacos, drizzle over roasted veggies, or serve as dips before dinner. It only took me another decade to realize that using jarred red peppers in this recipe is a million times easier and faster than roasting and peeling peppers yourself. I promise it doesn't alter the final outcome of the recipe enough to matter. Another bonus? The peppers are loaded with vitamin C!

GF | DF | *VG | V | Q! | MA

Prep: 10 minutes

Cook: 10 minutes

Makes 2 cups (480 ml)

2 tablespoons olive oil

½ cup (55 g) slivered almonds

1 small shallot, sliced

2 cloves garlic, coarsely chopped

Kosher salt

2 tablespoons fresh mint leaves

2 tablespoons fresh lime juice (about 1 lime)

Two 12-ounce (340-g) jars roasted red peppers, drained and rinsed

2 teaspoons honey or agave nectar

2 tablespoons hot pepper sauce, such as Tabasco or Siete (optional)

In a small skillet, heat the oil over medium heat and add the almonds. Toast, stirring frequently, until lightly browned, about 3 minutes. Add the shallot, garlic, and a pinch of salt. Stir until the shallot and garlic are fragrant, 30 to 60 seconds, then stir in the mint. Remove the mixture from the heat and add the lime juice carefully, as lime juice and oil can splatter when combined.

Let the mixture cool for a few minutes, then add to a blender or food processor along with the red peppers, honey, and hot sauce, if using. Blend until smooth. Taste, adding more salt as needed. Serve warm.

To store: Let cool completely and refrigerate in an airtight container for up to 5 days.

Classic Basil Pesto

The first time I made pesto was a life-changing experience for me as a cook. I could not believe that a few simple ingredients thrown into a food processor could produce a sauce that turned plain pasta, risotto, or a piece of fish or chicken into something so magical. The quality of the ingredients really matters here, as they have nothing to hide behind, so I use my favorite extra-virgin olive oil, bright green and fragrant basil, and real Parmigiano-Reggiano. Also, while I was consuming pounds of pesto in every restaurant I visited in and around Genoa, Italy, a chef gave me an earful, telling me to never toast the pine nuts, as pesto is a raw sauce that should not require cooking of any kind. Don't tell him, but I strongly disagree. Toasting the nuts adds a warmth and nuttiness to the sauce that I love. If you know anyone who refuses to eat green sauces, start them here. If they don't fall in love with pesto, I can't help you.

GF | V | Q! | MA

Prep: 15 minutes

Makes 1¼ cups (300 ml)

⅓ cup (45 g) pine nuts

⅓ cup (30 g) grated Parmesan cheese

2 cloves garlic

3 cups (90 g) firmly packed fresh basil leaves

½ cup (120 ml) extra-virgin olive oil, plus more to top sauce for storing

Kosher salt and freshly ground black pepper

TIP: Have a ton of basil and want to make a huge batch of pesto and freeze some? Do everything except add the Parmesan cheese, then freeze in covered ice cube trays or airtight containers. When ready to use, allow the pesto to defrost at room temperature before stirring in the cheese.

In a small, dry skillet, cook the pine nuts over medium heat, stirring constantly, until lightly browned and fragrant, 1 to 2 minutes. Transfer to a plate to cool completely.

In a food processor or blender, combine the cooled pine nuts, Parmesan, and garlic. Pulse a few times to break up the garlic. Add the basil and pulse an additional 10 to 15 times. With the motor running, slowly pour in the ½ cup (120 ml) olive oil and process until the pesto is the texture of a coarse paste. Add 2 tablespoons water and pulse to combine. Add more water, a tablespoon at a time, until the sauce reaches the desired consistency. Stir in ½ teaspoon salt and a few grindings of pepper. Taste and adjust the seasoning if needed.

To store: Refrigerate in an airtight container, topped with a thin layer of olive oil (pour a little over the back of a teaspoon), for up to 1 week.

Five-Spice BBQ Sauce

My mom made homemade barbecue sauce once a year to top the brisket that she served on Christmas Eve. Since red meat was something we ate only a handful of times a year when I was growing up, I remember sneaking into the foil-wrapped brisket while it was still in the oven to steal slices of the braised meat coated in this delightfully sweet barbecue sauce. I have made it slightly better for us by using ketchup free of refined sugar, and I ditched the liquid smoke. I also use a Chinese five-spice blend for a surprising twist on typical American barbecue sauce. This sauce is key to the Five-Star Five-Spice Ribs (page 181). If you are gluten-free, make sure to check the label on your Worcestershire sauce to make sure it's free of fillers.

GF | DF | *VG | *V | MA

Prep: 5 minutes

Cook: 25 minutes

Makes about 2 cups (480 ml)

1 tablespoon olive or avocado oil

½ cup (55 g) diced red onion

Kosher salt and freshly ground black pepper

1 cup (240 ml) sugar-free ketchup

1 cup (240 ml) water

1 to 2 tablespoons maple syrup

¼ cup (60 ml) Worcestershire sauce or vegan Worcestershire sauce

¼ cup (60 ml) apple cider vinegar

1 teaspoon Chinese five-spice powder

½ teaspoon onion powder

Hot pepper sauce (optional)

In a small saucepan, heat the oil over medium heat. Add the onion, a pinch of salt, and a few grinds of pepper. Cook, stirring occasionally, until the onion is soft and translucent, 5 to 8 minutes. Add the ketchup, water, maple syrup, Worcestershire sauce, vinegar, five-spice powder, and onion powder and bring to a boil. Reduce the heat to low and simmer until the sauce has thickened enough to coat the back of a spoon, 10 to 15 minutes. If desired, stir in a few teaspoons of hot sauce to reach the desired level of spiciness. Taste and adjust the salt as needed.

To store: Let cool completely. Refrigerate in an airtight container or containers for up to 1 week or freeze for up to 1 month.

Granch Dip

The name Granch is short for "Greek ranch." This dip is loaded with all of the fresh herbs and garlic we love, with a base of healthful Greek yogurt.

GF | V | Q! | MA

Prep: 5 minutes

Makes about 2 cups (480 ml)

1 pint (480 ml) Greek yogurt

3 tablespoons olive oil

2 tablespoons fresh lemon juice

2 cloves garlic, grated or minced

Kosher salt and freshly ground black pepper

¼ cup (12 g) assorted chopped fresh herbs, such as dill, mint, parsley, tarragon, and/or basil

Drain any liquid from the top of the yogurt, then transfer to a small bowl. Add the olive oil, lemon juice, and garlic and stir until well combined. Fold in the herbs, then season with salt and pepper to taste.

To store: Refrigerate in an airtight container for up to 1 week.

Classic Shallot Vinaigrette

If there is one thing I encourage you to make from scratch above all others, it's vinaigrette. When purchased at the store, it can be loaded with fillers, extra sodium, and sugar. Making one from scratch takes a matter of minutes, and the flavor is incomparable. Pick a recipe or two to make at the beginning of the week and use them any time you want a quick salad or have a go-to marinade for chicken or fish. The method for this and the vinaigrettes on the following pages is the same throughout. I've switched from making them in a bowl with a whisk to using a mason jar and shaking it with all of my body until the vinaigrette is perfectly emulsified. It's your choice.

GF | DF | *VG | V | Q! | MA

Prep: 10 minutes
Makes about ¾ cup (180 ml)

1 tablespoon minced shallot

2 teaspoons Dijon mustard

2 teaspoons honey or agave nectar

Kosher salt and freshly ground black pepper

¼ cup (60 ml) apple cider vinegar

½ cup (120 ml) extra-virgin olive oil

In a small mason jar or bowl, combine the shallot, mustard, honey, a pinch of salt, and a few grindings of pepper. Add the vinegar and shake or whisk to combine. Let sit for 5 minutes to allow the shallots to soften a bit in the vinegar. Add the olive oil and shake or whisk to combine. Taste, adding more seasoning if desired.

To store: Refrigerate in an airtight container for up to 1 week.

Balsamic Vinaigrette

GF | DF | VG | V | Q! | MA

Prep: 5 minutes
Makes 1 scant cup (240 ml)

2 tablespoons Dijon mustard

Kosher salt and freshly ground pepper

¼ cup (60 ml) balsamic vinegar

½ cup (120 ml) extra-virgin olive oil

In a small mason jar or bowl, combine the mustard, a pinch of salt, and a few grindings of pepper. Shake or whisk to combine, then add the vinegar and shake or whisk until smooth. Add the olive oil and shake or whisk to emulsify. Taste, adding more seasoning or oil if desired.

To store: Refrigerate in an airtight container for up to 1 week.

Lemon-Parmesan Vinaigrette

GF | DF | V | Q! | MA

Prep: 5 minutes
Makes 1 cup (240 ml)

1 tablespoon Dijon mustard

2 teaspoons minced garlic

¼ cup (60 ml) fresh lemon juice

¼ cup (25 g) grated Parmesan cheese

Kosher salt and ground pepper

½ cup (120 ml) extra-virgin olive oil

In a small mason jar or bowl, combine the mustard and garlic and shake or whisk to combine, then add the lemon juice, Parmesan, ½ teaspoon salt, and a few grindings of pepper. Shake or whisk again to combine. Add the olive oil and shake or whisk to emulsify. Taste, adding more salt or lemon juice if desired.

To store: Refrigerate in an airtight container for up to 5 days.

Curry-Lime Vinaigrette

GF | DF | VG | V | Q! | MA

Prep: 5 minutes

Makes about 1 cup (240 ml)

2 tablespoons minced shallot

1 tablespoon curry powder, plus more as needed

¼ cup (60 ml) fresh lime juice

1 teaspoon maple syrup

Kosher salt and freshly ground black pepper

½ cup (120 ml) avocado or olive oil

In a small mason jar or bowl, combine the shallot, the 1 tablespoon curry powder, the lime juice, maple syrup, ½ teaspoon salt, and a few grindings of pepper. Shake or whisk to combine. Add the oil and shake or whisk until emulsified.

To store: Refrigerate in an airtight container for up to 1 week.

Peanut Dressing

GF | DF | VG | V | Q! | MA

Prep: 15 minutes

Makes 1¼ to 1½ cups (300–360 ml)

½ cup (125 g) creamy peanut butter

½ cup (120 ml) fresh lime juice (about 4 limes)

¼ cup (50 g) lightly packed coconut sugar or light brown sugar

3 green onions, including white and light green parts, cut into 1-inch (2.5-cm) pieces

3 cloves garlic, crushed

1 teaspoon peeled and grated fresh ginger

⅓ cup (75 ml) toasted sesame oil

Kosher salt

In a blender, combine the peanut butter, lime juice, sugar, green onions, garlic, and ginger in a blender. Puree until smooth. Scrape down the sides with a rubber spatula. With the motor on low, slowly stream in the sesame oil, then add up to ½ cup (120 ml) water to reach the desired consistency. Taste, then season with salt.

Herby Green Goddess Dressing

This dressing is better for you than the typical Green Goddess, but it still has plenty of flavor. Tarragon is a classic herb for the dressing and I love it, but basil works just as well if you prefer.

GF | DF | V | Q! | MA

Prep: 10 minutes

Makes about 2 cups (480 ml)

2 tablespoons olive oil

1 tablespoon chopped shallot

2 cloves garlic, peeled

Kosher salt and freshly ground black pepper

1 cup (30 g) fresh flat-leaf parsley leaves

½ cup (15 g) fresh tarragon leaves

1 cup (240 ml) buttermilk

3 tablespoons mayonnaise or plain Greek yogurt

3 tablespoons fresh lemon juice

2 tablespoons finely chopped fresh chives

In a food processor or blender, combine the olive oil, shallot, garlic, ½ teaspoon salt, and ¼ teaspoon pepper. Pulse a few times to break up the garlic. Add the parsley and tarragon and pulse until coarsely chopped. Add the buttermilk, mayonnaise, and lemon juice. Blend until smooth. Taste, adding more salt to taste. Fold in the chives.

To store: Refrigerate in an airtight container for up to 1 week.

Chipotle-Lime Marinade

This marinade is equally good as a vinaigrette. In fact, I tend to make a double batch so I can use half for my Quinoa Salad with Chipotle-Lime Vinaigrette (page 107) and half as a marinade for chicken or shrimp, or even for corn, mushrooms, or squash when I want to grill up some vegetarian tacos.

GF | DF | *VG | V | Q! | MA

Prep: 10 minutes

Makes about 1 cup (240 ml)

½ cup (120 ml) fresh lime juice

3 tablespoons chopped canned chipotle chiles in adobo

¼ cup (30 g) diced red onion

2 tablespoons fresh mint leaves

2 tablespoons fresh cilantro leaves

2 tablespoons honey or agave nectar

3 cloves garlic, crushed

1 teaspoon dried oregano

1 teaspoon ground cumin

Kosher salt

½ cup (120 ml) avocado oil

In a blender, combine the lime juice, chipotle chiles and sauce, red onion, mint, cilantro, honey, garlic, oregano, cumin, and 1 teaspoon salt. Blend until it forms a paste and the garlic is broken up into small pieces. With the motor off, scrape down the sides of the blender, then add the oil. Blend until smooth. Add salt to taste, if needed.

To store: Refrigerate in an airtight container for up to 5 days.

Achiote Marinade

This is an abridged version of a marinade I learned to make for cochinita pibil, a Yucatán dish of pork baked in banana leaves. Achiote paste can be found in well-stocked markets or ordered online and is very inexpensive. I assure you it's worth the trouble!

GF | DF | VG | V | Q! | MA

Prep: 10 minutes
Makes about ½ cup (120 ml)

1 tablespoon achiote paste
2 teaspoons dried oregano
1 teaspoon ground cumin
½ teaspoon ground cloves
½ teaspoon freshly ground black pepper
4 tablespoons (60 ml) fresh lime juice
¼ cup (60 ml) fresh orange juice

In a small bowl, combine the achiote paste, oregano, cumin, cloves, and pepper. Break up the achiote paste with a fork if needed. Add 1 tablespoon of the lime juice, then whisk with the fork to form a smooth liquid. Add the remaining 3 tablespoons lime juice and the orange juice and whisk to combine.

To store: Refrigerate in an airtight container for up to 1 week.

Sesame-Asian Pear Marinade

When working on the marinades for this cookbook, I remembered a marinade my mom would make for chicken wings when I was little. It had five ingredients: soy sauce, sherry, brown sugar, a few knobs of ginger, and anise seeds. I realized my mom's recipe a was a simplified version of a marinade for Korean short ribs, or kalbi! The recipe here includes an Asian pear, as it has loads of flavor as well as enzymes that help tenderize the meat. (Fun trick, right?) If you can't find Asian pears, use a ripe Bosc pear as a substitute.

GF | DF | VG | V | Q! | MA

Prep: 10 minutes

Makes about 1 cup (240 ml)

1 small Asian pear (about 4 ounces/115 g), peeled, cored, and coarsely chopped

2 tablespoons light brown sugar or coconut sugar

2-inch (5-cm) piece fresh ginger, peeled

2 cloves garlic

¼ cup (60 ml) toasted sesame oil

¼ cup (60 ml) low-sodium tamari sauce

¼ cups (60 ml) sweet sherry or mirin

1 teaspoon anise seeds

In a food processor or blender, combine the pear, sugar, ginger, and garlic. Blend until a thick puree has formed. Add the sesame oil, tamari, sherry, and anise seeds and blend until smooth. If desired, strain the marinade before using.

To store: Refrigerate in an airtight container for up to 5 days.

Italian Seasoning

Spices are one of the best secrets to making dishes more healthful. Like herbs, each spice tends to have different health properties to aid digestion, reduce inflammation, and so much more. I call this one the holy trinity of Italian spice blends. It's absolutely delicious in pasta sauces, meatballs, and any braised dish you want to be extra-delicious. On the next few pages I've included more of my favorite combinations which I come back to time and time again. I recommend making a double or triple batch of any of these blends, then writing the name and date of the spice blend on your storage container.

GF | DF | VG | V | Q! | MA

Prep: 5 minutes

Makes about ¼ cup (9 g)

2 tablespoons fennel seeds

1 tablespoon dried oregano

¼ teaspoon red pepper flakes
(or less if you prefer less heat)

In a small jar, combine all of the spices and shake to blend.

To store: Cover tightly and keep in a cool, dark place for up to 1 month.

Moroccan Spice Blend

Warm spices mixed with the cumin and coriander create a depth of flavor that brings out the best of the simplest dishes. This blend works well with roasted chicken, lamb, and all kinds of vegetables.

GF | DF | VG | V | Q! | MA

Prep: 5 minutes

Makes about ¾ cup (72 g)

4 tablespoons ground cinnamon

2 tablespoons ground coriander

2 tablespoons ground turmeric

2 tablespoons ground cumin

1 tablespoon ground cardamom

1 teaspoon freshly ground black pepper

In a small jar, combine all of the spices.

To store: Cover tightly and keep in a cool, dark place for up to 1 month.

Autumn Spice Blend

I refuse to allow the Pumpkin Pie Spice Police to hijack these spices and claim they can be used just for products with the word *pumpkin* on the label. This blend is the backbone of my favorite fruit crisp recipe, my cashew milk recipe, and pretty much every recipe where I want the flavor and fragrance of warm spices for fall and winter.

GF | DF | VG | V | Q! | MA

Prep: 5 minutes

Makes about ¼ cup (24 g)

2 tablespoons ground cinnamon

1½ teaspoons ground ginger

1 teaspoon freshly ground nutmeg

1 teaspoon ground cloves

In a small jar, combine all of the spices and shake to blend.

To store: Refrigerate in an airtight container for up to 5 days.

Taco Spice Rub

I can turn anything into a taco. Grilled steak, chicken, shrimp, sweet potatoes, scrambled eggs—you name it and I'll put it in a tortilla and call it a meal! This spice blend adds the perfect amount of flavor to any ingredient you wish to add to your tacos.

GF | DF | VG | V | Q! | MA

Prep: 5 minutes

Makes about ¼ cup (24 g)

2 tablespoons chili powder

2 teaspoons ground cumin

2 teaspoons kosher salt

1 teaspoon garlic powder

1 teaspoon dried oregano

¼ teaspoon cayenne (optional)

In a small bowl, combine the chili powder, cumin, garlic powder, oregano, cayenne, and salt.

To store: Refrigerate in an airtight container for up to 3 months.

Techniques

TOASTING NUTS, COCONUT, AND SEEDS

To toast in the oven, preheat the oven to 350°F (175°C). Spread the nuts, coconut, or seeds on a parchment-lined baking sheet and bake, stirring once or twice, until lightly toasted and fragrant, 5 to 15 minutes.

To toast in a pan, in a large skillet over medium heat warm 1 tablespoon oil for each cup of nuts or seeds. Add the nuts or seeds to the pan with a generous pinch of salt. Toast, stirring constantly, until fragrant and lightly browned, 1 to 5 minutes. Transfer to a paper towel–lined plate to remove any excess oil before using.

MAKING BREAD CRUMBS

Cut bread into 2- to 3-inch (5- to 7.5-cm) pieces and leave out on the counter overnight. (If you prefer, remove the crust from the bread before using.) Pulse the pieces in a food processor until the crumbs reach a uniform size. Use immediately, or store in an airtight container in the freezer for up to 1 month.

TOASTING BREAD CRUMBS

In a large nonstick skillet over medium-high heat, warm 1 tablespoon olive oil or enough to cover the entire bottom of the skillet. Add 1 cup (45 g) coarse sourdough or country bread crumbs and a generous pinch of kosher salt. Toss to coat the crumbs with the oil. Cook, stirring frequently, until the crumbs are golden brown and lightly toasted on the outside, about 5 minutes. Using a slotted spoon, transfer to paper towels to drain.

TAMING ONIONS

To take the bite out of raw onions, slice them thinly, then submerge them in ice water for 10 minutes. Drain, pat dry with a paper towel, and add to your favorite recipe.

QUICK-SOAKING DRIED BEANS

If I remember and have the time, I like to soak dried beans overnight in cold water. But sometimes I just don't think about it! To shorten the soaking time, place dried beans in a pot and add cold water to cover. Bring the beans to a boil, immediately turn off the heat, and cover. Let sit for 1 hour, then drain the beans and proceed with the recipe.

HARD-BOILED EGGS

To hard-boil eggs, place up to 6 eggs in a medium saucepan and cover with cold water. Bring to a boil, then remove the pan from the heat and cover tightly with a lid. Allow the eggs to sit for 13 minutes. Immediately transfer the eggs to a bowl of ice water to chill.

Basically Breakfast

CHAPTER TWO

What I choose for breakfast sets the tone for my food choices for the rest of the day. It dictates my energy levels, too. When I start with refined carbohydrates, caffeine, and sugar, I'm zonked an hour later and left without energy or will power, craving the things I try to eat in moderation. So, whether you have five minutes or twenty to make breakfast, these recipes are designed to be the fuel you need to start your day. I like to start my day with good sources of protein, fruits, and vegetables, and go light on the starch. I stay fuller longer, and eating protein and veggies first prevents a spike in blood sugar. The breakfast tacos come together in a matter of minutes, but would be delicious for brunch or lunch, too. The egg bites are easy to reheat and eat on the run, the savory oats (with or without the egg) are amazing when you have ten minutes to enjoy them, and the scones and pancakes will knock your socks off as a weekend treat.

Breakfast Tacos

If you love big breakfasts, this one will become an all-time favorite! It's a classic "basically better-for-you" recipe: The fiber in the beans will keep you fueled through the morning, and the combination of avocado, black beans, and cheesy eggs is delicious. If you're used to relying on bacon or sausage as your big flavor bombs at breakfast, you won't miss either of them here! Also, I always use store-bought pico de gallo that you can find in the refrigerated section in the produce aisle. Full of freshly chopped tomatoes, onions, lime juice, and a little jalapeno, it's the perfect condiment to wake up your eggs, burritos, potatoes, or anything where regular salsa is used.

GF | V | Q!

Prep: 15 minutes

Cook: 10 minutes

Makes 4 servings

One 15-ounce (430-g) can no-salt-added black beans, drained and rinsed

2 teaspoons fresh lime juice

8 large eggs, lightly beaten

⅔ cup (2 ounces/55 g) shredded Cheddar cheese

Kosher salt

8 small (4-inch/10-cm) corn tortillas

1 cup (240 ml) purchased pico de gallo or your favorite salsa

1 ripe avocado, pitted, peeled, and cut into 8 slices

Fresh cilantro sprigs, for garnish

Lime wedges, for serving

In a small bowl, combine the beans and lime juice. Mash the beans with the back of a spoon until almost smooth.

Heat a large nonstick skillet over medium-low heat, then spray lightly with cooking spray. Add the eggs and cook, without stirring, until they start to set on the bottom. Draw a wooden spatula across the bottom of the pan to form curds, scraping it gently across the entire bottom of the pan. Continue cooking, stirring occasionally, until the eggs are set but not dry. Remove from the pan immediately and stir in half of the cheese. Season with a pinch of salt.

Wipe the skillet clean, then place it over medium heat and coat the pan with cooking spray. Add the tortillas to the pan in 2 batches. Heat them for 20 seconds on each side or just until soft. Remove from the pan and keep warm in a kitchen towel while assembling the tacos.

To serve, place two warm tortillas on each plate. Spread some of the black bean mixture across the center of each tortilla. Top each with the eggs, salsa, and cheese, dividing evenly between the tortillas. Top each taco with an avocado slice and garnish with the cilantro. Serve at once, with the lime wedges alongside.

Veggie Scramble with Goat Cheese

I'm convinced that most restaurants created veggie scrambles to use up the left-over side-dish offerings from the night before. But since I love scrambled eggs, I wanted to create a combination that is absolutely craveable! I love how goat cheese melts into eggs, and my culinary assistant, Caitlin, suggested adding corn and spinach as the veggies. We used fresh thyme as the herb of choice, and when I tasted this scramble I said, "Yep, that's what I want!" You can use raw, cooked, or defrosted frozen corn kernels. Just make sure you've allowed frozen kernels to defrost thoroughly so they don't add extra liquid to the pan.

GF | V | Q!

Prep: 5 minutes

Cook: 15 minutes

Makes 4 servings

1 tablespoon olive oil

½ cup (55 g) diced yellow onion

Kosher salt

1 cup (30 g) chopped spinach or chard leaves, firmly packed

½ cup (75 g) fresh or defrosted frozen corn kernels

8 large eggs, lightly beaten

2 ounces (55 g) crumbled fresh goat cheese

½ teaspoon finely chopped fresh thyme

Freshly ground black pepper

In a large nonstick pan, heat the olive oil over medium heat. Add the onion and a pinch of salt. Cook, stirring occasionally, until the onion is soft, about 8 minutes. Add the spinach, corn, and another generous pinch of salt and cook, stirring, until the spinach is just wilted, about 2 minutes. Add the eggs and cook without stirring until the eggs start to set when you run a wooden spatula along the bottom of the pan. Continue cooking, stirring frequently, until the eggs are fully cooked but still moist, 1 to 2 minutes.

Remove the pan from the heat. Stir in the goat cheese and thyme. Season with salt and pepper and serve at once.

Green Eggs and Ham (Mini Baked Egg Muffins)

Bacon is one of my favorite foods on earth, but after a few doctors informed me that it's never going to be on a list of healthful foods to eat, I'm trying to find ways to enjoy the flavor of bacon while eating less of it. This recipe is absolutely perfect because I can get my bacon fix without overdoing it. The best part about these egg bites is that you can make them your own. Substitute cream cheese or Swiss for the Cheddar, or leave out the bacon and replace it with any veggie you like!

GF

Prep: 15 minutes

Cook: 15 minutes

Makes 12 mini muffins

4 ounces (115 g) thick-sliced bacon (about 4 slices), diced

8 large eggs

½ cup (120 ml) heavy cream

4 ounces (115 g) shredded Cheddar cheese

¼ cup (10 g) thinly sliced fresh basil leaves

Kosher salt and freshly ground black pepper

2 tablespoons pesto, home-made (page 51) or store-bought, for garnish (optional)

Spray the cups of a 12-cup standard muffin pan generously with cooking spray. Preheat the oven to 350°F (175°C).

Heat a medium nonstick skillet over medium heat. Add the bacon and cook, stirring frequently, until fully cooked and crispy, about 5 minutes. In a fine-mesh sieve placed over a bowl, drain the bacon, then discard the fat or save it for another use. Transfer the bacon to a paper towel to continue to absorb the fat.

In a large bowl, whisk together the eggs and cream until frothy. Add the cheese, basil, ½ teaspoon salt, and ¼ teaspoon pepper. Stir to combine.

Divide the bacon evenly among the muffin cups, then divide the egg mixture among the cups. They should be about two-thirds full.

Bake until the eggs have puffed up and set and are beginning to brown, 18 to 20 minutes. Let cool in the pan for a few minutes, then remove from the pan. Garnish with the pesto, if using, and serve.

To store: Let cool completely and refrigerate in an airtight container for up to 4 days. Reheat in a microwave for 30 seconds or in a preheated 300°F (150°C) oven for 5 minutes.

Savory Steel-Cut Oats with Greens and Prosciutto

Okay, let's talk about savory oats. I have to credit my editor, Kim Laidlaw, with this idea. I love steel-cut oats, but I usually pile mine high with butter, brown sugar, and cinnamon. (Yes, they're delicious.) But when Kim said, "What about savory oats?" I started daydreaming about the combination below. Cooking the oats in my Change-Your-Life Chicken Stock (page 43) was indeed life-changing, but you can certainly cook them in water, veggie stock (page 44), or even milk if you prefer. The sautéed greens and sunny-side up egg take this breakfast dish from simple to fabulous, and a few slices of prosciutto draped over the top makes it straight-up sexy.

GF | DF

Prep: 10 minutes

Cook: 25 minutes

Makes 4 servings

3½ cups (840 ml) chicken stock (page 43), vegetable stock (page 44), or water

1 cup (155 g) gluten-free steel-cut oats, such as Bob's Red Mill

Kosher salt

4 thin slices prosciutto (about 1¼ ounces/35 g total)

3 cups (90 g) firmly packed chopped greens, such as chard or spinach leaves

4 large eggs

Freshly ground black pepper

TIP: Love steel-cut oats for breakfast? Make a double batch on the weekend, let cool, then refrigerate them in an airtight container. The leftover oats will reheat well in a microwave with just a splash of water added to them.

In a medium saucepan, bring the stock to a boil over medium-high heat. Add the oats and a pinch of salt. Reduce the heat to low, cover, and simmer, stirring occasionally, until the oats are tender, about 20 minutes, adding a little more liquid if necessary until the oats are cooked. Taste, adding more salt if necessary.

Meanwhile, heat a large nonstick skillet over medium-high heat. Add the prosciutto to the skillet and cook until crispy on both sides, flipping halfway, 5 to 6 minutes. Remove from the skillet and set aside.

Reduce the heat to medium. Add the greens to the skillet with a pinch of salt. Cook, stirring occasionally, until wilted, 2 to 6 minutes, depending on the types of greens used. Remove from the pan, squeeze out any excess liquid in a paper towel, and set aside. Pour out any excess liquid from the pan and wipe with a paper towel.

Spray the skillet lightly with cooking spray. One at a time, crack the eggs into the pan, spacing them about 2 inches (5 cm) apart. Cover and cook until the egg whites are set and no longer runny, about 2 minutes. Season each egg with salt and pepper.

Divide the oats equally among 4 shallow bowls. Top with the greens, dividing evenly between the bowls, then top each with an egg. Season with salt and pepper. Top each bowl with a piece of prosciutto and serve right away.

Build-Your-Own Spiced Chia Puddings

Chia seeds are all the rage in the wellness world, and with good reason. They are full of fiber, which can help reduce your risk of heart disease and high blood pressure. They can also improve digestive health and metabolism. It's easy to make these "puddings," as no cooking is required! When given time to absorb the liquid they're soaking in, the seeds become gelatinous and are delicious served with a little honey or maple syrup and fresh fruit. Once you master the technique—so simple!—you can add any toppings you like to boost flavor and texture. (My favorite topping combinations are given at the end of the recipe.) The homemade cashew milk is perfect in these puddings, but you can also use coconut milk; just be sure to choose a light version because full-fat coconut milk is too heavy.

GF | DF | VG | V | MA

Prep: 10 minutes

Chill: Overnight or for up to 18 hours

Makes 2 to 3 servings

2 cups (480 ml) Vanilla-Spice Cashew Milk (page 79) or light coconut milk

6 tablespoons (70 g) chia seeds

1 tablespoon maple syrup or honey

¼ teaspoon Autumn Spice Blend (page 64) or ground cinnamon

Kosher salt

Toppings (see right)

In a 3- to 4-cup (720- to 960-ml) container with a tight-fitting lid, combine the milk, chia seeds, maple syrup, spice blend, and a generous pinch of salt. Cover and shake to combine. Chill for 2 hours, then remove from the fridge and shake the pudding or whisk it vigorously to break up any clumps of seeds. Chill for an additional 8 to 12 hours.

When ready to eat, scoop out a portion and top with your favorite combination of fruit, nuts, and/or seeds.

SUGGESTED TOPPINGS

- Dried unsweetened cherries, toasted walnuts, and a drizzle of maple syrup
- Fresh blueberries, fresh blackberries, and grated lemon zest
- Granola and toasted coconut flakes
- Dark chocolate chunks and chopped toasted almonds
- Sliced fresh strawberries and a sprinkle of brown sugar

Gluten-Free Lemon-Currant Scones

Without gluten in my life, I still dream about a few foods I can no longer enjoy: a slice of Zachary's deep-dish pizza in Oakland, California; a turkey sandwich with thick slices of toasted homemade whole-wheat bread; and the perfect morning bun. But we've made so much progress in the world of gluten-free flour blends that I decided it was time to start re-creating some of my favorite treats. This is my favorite scone flavor of all time—there's just something irresistible about the currants and the lemon zest.

GF | V | MA

Prep: 25 minutes

Cook: 18 to 20 minutes

Makes 8 scones

½ cup (70 g) dried currants

2 cups (250 g) gluten-free flour blend, such as Bob's Red Mill 1-to-1 Baking Flour

1 tablespoon baking powder

¼ cup (50 g) sugar

½ teaspoon kosher salt

10 tablespoons (135 g) cold unsalted butter, cut into 1-tablespoon slices

½ cup (120 ml) 2 percent milk or full-fat nut milk

1 large egg, lightly beaten

1 tablespoon finely grated fresh lemon zest

1 tablespoon turbinado sugar, for garnish (optional)

Preheat the oven to 400°F (205°C). Line a baking sheet with parchment paper.

Put the currants in a small bowl of warm water for 10 minutes to rehydrate, then drain and pat dry with a paper towel.

Meanwhile, in a large bowl, combine the flour, baking powder, sugar, and salt. Stir with a whisk to blend. Add 8 tablespoons (115 g) of the cubed butter to the bowl. Working quickly, use your hands to crumble the butter and flour mixture together until the butter pieces are pea sized.

Add the milk, egg, and lemon zest to the flour mixture. Using a rubber spatula, stir the wet ingredients into the dry ingredients until just combined, being careful to not overmix. Stir in the currants.

Turn the dough out onto a lightly floured cutting board. Use your hands to gently form the dough into a round about 8 inches (20 cm) in diameter and 2 inches (5 cm) thick. Cut the dough into quarters, then cut each piece in half so you have 8 triangular scones. Place the scones on the baking sheet about 2 inches (5 cm) apart. Put the baking sheet in the freezer for 10 minutes to chill.

Meanwhile, melt the remaining 2 tablespoons butter. Remove the scones from the freezer and brush with the melted butter, then sprinkle each scone with the turbinado sugar (if using).

Bake for 18 to 20 minutes, or until lightly golden. Serve hot.

To store: Let cool completely on a wire rack, then refrigerate in a resealable storage bag for up to 2 days. Reheat in a preheated 300°F (150°C) oven for 5 to 8 minutes.

Gluten-Free Pancakes with Berry Compote

I love pancakes and waffles and usually don't bother making them from scratch, but once again, this book inspired me to see how long it takes to make a better-for-you version of a family favorite. Most popular mixes are loaded with preservatives. Once I realized how easy these are to whip up, I'll never buy boxed mix again!

GF | V | Q!

Prep: 5 minutes

Cook: 15 minutes

Makes 4 servings

BERRY COMPOTE

2 cups (280 g) fresh or frozen mixed berries

¼ cup (60 ml) maple syrup

PANCAKES

1 cup (125 g) gluten-free flour blend, such as Bob's Red Mill 1-to-1 Baking Flour

1 tablespoon baking powder

¼ teaspoon kosher salt

1 cup (240 ml) whole milk or unsweetened plant-based milk

1 large egg, lightly beaten

1 tablespoon honey, warmed

For the compote: in a small saucepan over medium-low heat, combine the berries and maple syrup. Simmer, stirring occasionally, until juicy and slightly thickened, about 10 minutes for frozen berries, 5 to 8 minutes for fresh. Break the berries up slightly with a fork as they are cooking.

Meanwhile, for the pancakes, in a medium bowl, whisk the flour, baking powder, and salt to blend. In a small bowl, whisk the milk and egg until smooth, then whisk in the honey. Add the milk mixture to the flour mixture and stir until the mix is slightly lumpy, making sure not to overmix.

Heat a large nonstick skillet over medium heat. Spray the pan lightly with cooking spray. Using a ¼-cup (60-ml) measure, add batter to make 2 to 4 small pancakes, depending on the size of your pan. Cook until the pancakes form bubbles around the edges and are golden on the bottom, then flip and cook until cooked through, about 4 minutes total. Serve at once, with berry compote spooned over.

Better-for-You Granola

Many of the ingredients in granola can be great for your health! Nuts, seeds, and oats provide us with loads of protein, vitamin B6, vitamin E, zinc, and plant-based omega-3 fatty acids. (A handful of nuts a day can help lower blood sugar levels, improve cholesterol, and aid digestion.) But most commercial granolas also contain quite a bit of sugar. So instead of using sugar in this recipe, I use the smallest amount of maple syrup possible to add some flavor while allowing the other ingredients to shine! The egg whites are used to help create clumps of granola. If you prefer to omit them, you'll still enjoy all of the flavors but with fewer chunks. Oats are naturally gluten-free but are often processed in mills where they can be contaminated with gluten, so if necessary, look for a brand that is certified gluten-free.

GF | DF | *VG | V | MA

Prep: 10 minutes

Cook: 25 minutes

Makes 7 cups (725 g); serves 10 to 12

4 cups (360 g) gluten-free old-fashioned rolled oats, such as Bob's Red Mill brand

1 cup (95 g) sliced almonds

1 cup (130 g) pumpkin seeds

1 cup (140 g) sunflower seeds

1 teaspoon Autumn Spice Blend (page 64)

1 teaspoon kosher salt

¼ cup (60 ml) coconut oil, melted and cooled slightly

2 egg whites, beaten until frothy (optional)

2 tablespoons maple syrup

Position a rack in the center of the oven and preheat the oven to 350°F (175°C). Line a baking sheet with parchment paper.

In a large bowl, combine the oats, almonds, pumpkin seeds, sunflower seeds, spice blend, and salt. Add the oil, egg whites, and maple syrup and stir well. Spread the oat mixture evenly onto the prepared pan and bake until golden, stirring the granola with a rubber spatula and rotating the pan halfway through, 20 to 25 minutes.

Remove the granola from the oven and let cool completely; it will crisp up as it cools.

To store: Store in an airtight container at room temperature for up to 1 month.

Vanilla-Spice Cashew Milk

Cow's milk and I have had an on-again/off-again relationship for most of my adult life. I absolutely love it, but it refuses to love me back. After years of adding sad dairy replacements to my coffee, I finally decided to try making my own nut milks. The almond milk I made was good but terribly time-consuming to make, and now we know how taxing almonds are on our water supply. Cashews, however, can become milk in a matter of minutes, and the texture is creamy and satisfying. The milk will separate while stored in the fridge, so give it a good shake each time before using.

GF | DF | VG | V | MA

Prep: 10 minutes, plus 20 minutes to soak

Makes 6 to 7 cups (1.4 to 1.7 l)

2 cups (240 g) unsalted raw cashews

6 cups (1.4 l) filtered water

2 to 4 tablespoons maple syrup (optional)

1 tablespoon Autumn Spice Blend (page 64)

NOTE: For unsweetened cashew milk, omit the maple syrup and the spices and add a generous pinch of sea salt to the mixture.

Put the cashews and 2 cups (480 ml) of the water in a blender. Let soak for 20 minutes.

Add 2 tablespoons of the maple syrup (if using) and the spice blend. Blend at low speed, then slowly increase the speed to high and blend until smooth. Add the remaining 4 cups (960 ml) water and the remaining 2 tablespoons maple syrup (if desired) to reach your preferred consistency and taste.

Pour the cashew milk through a sieve and discard the solids. Transfer to an airtight container and store in the refrigerator for up to 4 days, making sure to stir or shake the milk each time before serving.

(Actually) Delicious Green Juice

I go through phases where I'll make fresh juices every day, then I lose my thunder. Let's face it, the prep and cleanup time is REAL. But whenever my body hurts more than usual, I take up juicing again. I treat it like a new hobby and commit to doing it once a day. Guess what happens? I always feel better when I include fresh juice in my diet. If you're new to juicing, stick to the 80/20 rule: 80 percent vegetables and 20 percent fruit. Depending on the type of juicer you use, you may be losing lots of the valuable fiber we get when eating fruit whole, so it's a great rule of thumb when starting. Also, turmeric is a wildly effective anti-inflammatory ingredient, but if you use it, make sure to add a few grindings of black pepper to your juice. No joke! It increases the bioavailability of the turmeric by 200 percent!

GF | DF | VG | V | Q!

Prep: 15 minutes

Makes 4 cups (960 ml)

6 stalks organic celery

2 large organic English cucumbers

2 organic Granny Smith apples

½ bunch organic fresh flat-leaf parsley

2-inch (5-cm) piece organic fresh ginger

2-inch (5-cm) piece organic fresh turmeric

Juice of 1 lemon or lime

Freshly ground black pepper

Wash all the fruits and vegetables and pat dry. In a juicer, juice the celery, cucumbers, apples, parsley, ginger, and turmeric according to the juicer manufacturer's instructions. Add the lemon juice and a few grindings of black pepper. Stir well.

The juice is at its most potent when consumed immediately, but the remaining juice can be stored in an airtight container in the refrigerator for up to 3 days.

Chunky Monkey Smoothie

My sons are practically adults now, and they still love smoothies. But now that they both drive and can buy commercial smoothies (like gummy candy–flavored ones!) that are basically over-the-top sugar bombs, I came up with this healthful version to serve at home.

GF | DF | VG | V | Q!

Prep: 15 minutes

Makes 1 smoothie

1 frozen banana, cut into pieces (see Note)

2 tablespoons unsweetened almond butter or peanut butter

2 tablespoons cacao powder, such as Navitas

1 tablespoon maple syrup

1 teaspoon vanilla extract

1 cup (240 ml) Vanilla-Spice Cashew Milk (page 79), or your favorite plant-based milk

1 cup (215 g) ice cubes

NOTE: To freeze bananas, peel them and cut into 2-inch (5-cm) pieces, then place in a sealable storage bag. Push the air out as you seal it, then freeze for up to 2 weeks. Pull out pieces as you need them.

In a high-speed blender, combine the banana pieces, almond butter, cacao powder, maple syrup, and vanilla. Pour the milk over the top. Blend on medium-low speed to break up the big chunks of banana. Add the ice and blend on high speed until smooth. Serve at once.

Açaí Berry Blast

Açaí berries have been deemed a superfood for many reasons. Loaded with omega fats, protein, and fiber, they have more antioxidants than blueberries or pomegranates. Crazy, right? Grown mainly in the Amazon rainforest, the berries have to be pureed and frozen because they are highly perishable. Most of the brands sold in the United States are organic and typically come in 3½-ounce (100-g) packets. Before putting them in the blender, let a packet soften in a bowl of warm water for a few minutes before opening. And since these berries have very little natural sugar, using frozen mango as the other fruit adds a punch of natural sweetness.

GF | DF | VG | V | Q!

Prep: 15 minutes

Makes 2 smoothies

One 3½-ounce (100-g) package frozen unsweetened açaí puree

1 cup (165 g) frozen mango chunks

½ cup (75 g) frozen mixed berries

1 to 2 teaspoons maple syrup

2 cups (480 ml) Vanilla-Spice Cashew Milk (page 79), or your favorite plant-based milk

½ teaspoon vanilla extract (optional)

In a blender, combine the açaí puree, mango chunks, berries, and 1 teaspoon maple syrup. Add the milk and vanilla (if using) and blend until smooth. Taste and add 1 more teaspoon maple syrup, if desired. Serve at once.

TIP: To store any left-over smoothie, pour the remaining smoothie into an ice cube tray. Cover tightly with plastic wrap and freeze. When ready to serve, pop out a few cubes and blend again.

Simply
Snacks

CHAPTER THREE

I f I'm eating meals that are full of ingredients that make me feel great, I don't usually need much of a snack. However, my kids still tend to want something substantial if they're playing sports, and sometimes I get hungry around 4 or 5 p.m. and decide I'd like to turn my snack into an early dinner. From Everything Popcorn (page 95) to a Paint-by-Numbers Snack Board (page 87), you'll be ready to curb any craving for simple carbs, fats, and sugars with something easy and better for you.

Paint-by-Numbers Snack Board with Crudités and Dips

Cheese and charcuterie to veggies and dip—snack boards are such a fun way to eat! You can build a board with practically any finger food, squeezing in everyone's favorite ingredients. Not sure how to make your board look good? Treat it like a paint-by-number picture. The most important tip? Remove any space between ingredients. It will make the board appear abundant.

GF | V | Q!

Prep: 20 minutes
Makes 8 to 10 servings

Granch Dip (page 53)

Cheater Romesco (page 50)

Assorted olives and nuts

1 small jar honey or fruit preserves

8 to 12 small carrots, peeled

2 bunches radishes, stemmed

1 red bell pepper, seeded and cut into strips

3 mini cucumbers, sliced into 1-inch (2.5-cm) diagonal pieces

Assorted crackers

2 or 3 cheeses, such as Gouda, goat, blue, or Cheddar

To build the board, put the dip, romesco sauce, olives, nuts, and honey or preserves in separate small bowls.

Arrange the bowls and all the other ingredients on a large cutting board, packing all of the ingredients in tightly so the board is full.

Place any cutlery or necessary spoons around the board for serving. Serve with small plates and napkins.

Mexican Street Corn-off-the-Cob Dip

With all of the intense flavors of esquites, this dip is great served with tortilla chips, as a side salad with chicken or ribs, or as a topping for tacos. Here, the corn is grilled over a charcoal or wood fire, but you can also char it on a stove-top grill pan or under the broiler.

GF | V

Prep: 15 minutes

Cook: 15 to 30 minutes

Makes 6 to 8 servings

6 ears corn, shucked

Olive oil, for brushing

1 tablespoon Tajín seasoning, chili powder, or pure chile powder

Kosher salt

1 cup (240 ml) Mexican crema, crème fraîche, or sour cream

Grated zest and juice of 1 lime (2 tablespoons lime juice), plus more if desired

4 tablespoons (10 g) chopped fresh cilantro

½ cup (60 g) crumbled cotija cheese

¼ cup (35 g) minced red or white onion

½ pint (145 g) cherry tomatoes, halved

1 ripe avocado, pitted, peeled, and diced (optional)

Prepare a grill for direct cooking over medium-high heat (450°F/230°C). Brush the grill grate clean.

Brush the corn with olive oil, then sprinkle the Tajín seasoning evenly on all sides of the corn. If using pure chile powder, sprinkle the corn with 1 teaspoon salt as well. Grill the corn, turning once or twice while cooking, until charred and crisp-tender. Depending on the type of grill, this will take 15 to 30 minutes.

In a large bowl, whisk together the crema, lime zest, and lime juice. Add 3 tablespoons of the cilantro, the cotija cheese, and the onion to the crema mixture. Stir to combine.

Cut the kernels off the cobs and transfer to the bowl with the crema mixture. Stir gently to coat the corn. Add the cherry tomatoes and avocado, if using. Taste, adding more salt, Tajín seasoning, and/or lime juice if desired. Top with the remaining 1 tablespoon cilantro and serve.

Classic Cheese and Charcuterie Board

Cheese and charcuterie boards reign supreme when I entertain. If my friends show up hungry, they can dig right in. Depending on the type of meal I'm making for dinner, I'll vary the foods for the board so my guests don't get too full before the main event. When focusing on cheeses and charcuterie, I recommend choosing three different cheeses that vary in texture and flavor and including a fan favorite or two. Everyone tends to go straight for the triple creams (like Brie), and I love serving a hard cheese like Manchego or Gouda with something sweet like fruit preserves or slices of apple.

For the charcuterie, I stick to one or two types, usually an Italian fennel or calabrese sausage that I can slice into pieces, and then a prosciutto or salami that has already been cut into very thin slices. It's a nice combination of textures. Complete your board with crackers, slices of apples or pears, grapes in clusters, and your other favorite snack items, like Marcona almonds or your favorite type of olive.

GF | Q!

Prep: 20 minutes

Makes 4 to 6 servings

3 cheeses, such as Brie, goat cheese, blue cheese, Gouda, Swiss, and/or Cheddar

2 types thinly sliced salami

1 jar honey or fig jam

Almonds or sweetened walnuts

Olives

Crackers

Fruit, such as sliced apples or pears, or clusters of grapes

Chunks of dark chocolate

TIP: If serving olives or any fruit with pits, make sure to place a small bowl next to that ingredient, so guests have a place to discard their pits. Place one in the bowl to prompt them.

Unwrap the cheeses and salami and allow them to come to room temperature for 30 minutes. Put the jam, almonds, and olives into separate small bowls. Place all the ingredients on a cutting board, making sure to pack them closely together so the board is full and abundant. Place the appropriate knives and spoons around the board where needed for slicing cheese or scooping up ingredients. Serve with cocktail plates and napkins.

Basically Better Spinach and Artichoke Dip

Spinach-artichoke dip is what dreams are made of. My mom was a health nut when I was growing up, rarely allowing us to eat red meat, full-fat cheeses, or sugar. But my Aunt Betsy would make the most delicious spinach-artichoke dip for me. One time, I stood by the dip and ate the entire thing while my cousins were playing outside. I was strangely proud of my accomplishment. No, I would not recommend trying that one yourself, but I do recommend making this better version of the classic dip. I've cut down on the high-fat ingredients of the original, while keeping all of the flavor and ooey, gooey goodness of melty cheese. You can enjoy a serving of this delicious dip knowing that there are some actual health benefits to enjoy along with the amazing flavor!

GF | V

Prep: 20 minutes

Cook: 25 minutes

Makes 8 to 12 servings

2 tablespoons olive oil

1 yellow onion, diced (about 2 cups/220 g)

Kosher salt

2 cloves garlic, minced

One 14-ounce (400-g) can artichoke hearts, drained

One 16-ounce (455-g) package frozen chopped spinach, defrosted, excess liquid squeezed out (see Tip)

1 cup (8½ ounces/240 g) fresh goat cheese

2 cups (5 ounces/140 g) shredded Gruyère

¼ cup (60 ml) mayonnaise or plain Greek yogurt

1 tablespoon fresh lemon juice mixed with 2 teaspoons hot sauce (optional)

¼ cup (25 g) grated Parmesan cheese

Crackers, carrot sticks, celery sticks, or crostini, for serving

Preheat the oven to 350°F (175°C). Lightly coat an 8-inch (20-cm) square baking pan or oval baker with nonstick cooking spray.

In a medium skillet, heat the olive oil over medium heat. Add the onion and a pinch of salt and cook, stirring frequently, until softened, 5 to 8 minutes. Stir in the garlic and cook until fragrant, about 1 minute. Remove from the heat and set aside to cool.

In the bowl of a food processor, combine the artichoke hearts, spinach, goat cheese, 1 cup (70 g) Gruyère, mayonnaise, the lemon juice–hot sauce mixture (if using), and a pinch of salt. Process until smooth or leave it a little chunky if preferred. Add the onion mixture and pulse a few more times to combine. Taste and season with salt if needed. Transfer the mixture to the prepared baking dish.

Sprinkle with the remaining 1 cup (70 g) Gruyère, then the Parmesan. Bake until the dip is heated through and the cheese on the edges is just beginning to brown, 20 to 25 minutes. Turn the broiler to high and broil for another 2 to 5 minutes, or until the cheese on top is golden brown and bubbly.

Serve warm, with crackers, carrot or celery sticks, or crostini.

TIP: To remove excess liquid from defrosted frozen spinach (there will be a lot), place the defrosted spinach across the shorter end of a clean kitchen towel, leaving a little space on each side. Roll the spinach up into the towel, pressing on it every few rolls so the towel can absorb the water. When the towel is fully rolled, twist the ends like a Tootsie Roll to remove any remaining liquid.

Flatbread Two Ways

If you love impromptu dinners or drinks with friends and family, it's always great to keep a few balls of pizza dough in the freezer or the fridge. Besides using them to make pizza, you can roll them out and turn them into any type of flatbread to load with your favorite toppings. Here are two combos that are simple yet dressed to impress!

GF | DF | V

Prep: 10 minutes (plus 30 minutes for resting)

Cook: 15 minutes

Makes about 6 servings

1 pound (455 g) store-bought pizza dough, halved

Olive oil

Kosher salt

1 pint (290 g) cherry tomatoes, halved

4 ounces (115 g) fresh mozzarella, patted dry and torn into bite-size pieces

1 teaspoon chopped fresh oregano, plus more for garnish

3 tablespoons fig jam

4 ounces (115 g) Brie cheese, sliced

1½ cups (30 g) arugula

2 ounces (55 g) thinly sliced prosciutto, torn into pieces

> **TIP:** If storing the pizza dough in the freezer, place it in the refrigerator to start defrosting the night before using. The day you'd like to use it, place it on the counter at room temperature in the morning. Refrigerated dough will stay fresh for 2 days.

Place each ball of dough on a lightly floured surface. Let the dough rest at room temperature for 30 minutes.

Position 2 oven racks evenly in the oven and preheat to 450°F (230°C). Line two rimmed baking sheets with parchment paper.

Lightly dust each ball of dough with flour, then roll each one into a large rectangle about 13 by 7 (33 by 17 cm) inches. Transfer each rectangle to a prepared pan. Brush each piece of dough with ½ tablespoon olive oil and sprinkle with a pinch of salt.

Bake the dough until light golden bubbles form on the top and bottom, 10 to 12 minutes.

While the flatbread bakes, combine the cherry tomatoes, mozzarella, oregano, 1 tablespoon olive oil, and a pinch of salt in a medium bowl. Taste, adding more salt if necessary.

Remove the flatbreads from the oven and place on a serving tray or cutting board. Spoon the tomato mixture over the first flatbread, then sprinkle with a little more oregano to garnish.

Spread the fig jam over the other flatbread, then arrange the Brie in an even layer on top of the jam.

Toss the arugula with a teaspoon of olive oil and a pinch of salt, then top the fig pizza with the arugula and prosciutto pieces.

Slice the flatbreads and serve immediately.

Chipotle-Lime Wings

I never tire of my chipotle-lime marinade, as it's delicious as a dressing for green salads or Quinoa Salad (page 107) and as a marinade or sauce for chicken. Dredging the chicken wings in cornstarch gives them a wonderfully crispy coating, and as soon as they come out of the oven, they're tossed in the marinade. I dare you to stop at just a few!

GF | DF

Prep: 15 minutes

Cook: 30 minutes

Makes 6 servings

3 pounds (1.4 kg) chicken wings

2 tablespoons cornstarch

1 teaspoon kosher salt

½ cup (120 ml) Chipotle-Lime Marinade (page 59)

Preheat the oven to 425°F (220°C). Line a baking sheet with aluminum foil and place a wire rack on top. Spray the rack with cooking spray.

If you bought whole chicken wings, cut off the wing tips and separate the drumettes from the wings. Pat them dry. Discard the wing tips or save them for chicken stock.

In a medium bowl, combine the cornstarch and a pinch of salt. Add the wings to the bowl and toss well to combine. Spread the wings out on the baking rack.

Bake until the chicken is crispy on top, about 30 minutes. Flip the wings and bake until the wings are crispy all over and cooked through, about 15 minutes longer.

Transfer the hot wings to a large, wide bowl and drizzle with the marinade. Toss to coat evenly. Serve hot.

Everything Popcorn

I absolutely love popcorn and usually serve it buttered and lightly salted or tossed with cinnamon sugar. But when thinking about new ideas for this book, I remembered the beloved "everything bagel" and turned this popcorn into a similar treat. This version is better for you than any commercial seasoned popcorn, and it's more fun, too!

GF | V | Q!

Prep: 5 minutes

Cook: 5 minutes

Makes 4 servings

2 tablespoons avocado or coconut oil

½ cup (65 g) popcorn kernels

4 tablespoons (55 g) unsalted butter, melted

¼ cup (25 g) grated Parmesan

2 tablespoons "Everything Bagel" seasoning

Kosher salt

In a large saucepan over medium-high heat, add the oil and a few kernels of popcorn and cover. Once the sample kernels pop, add the remaining kernels, cover again, and give the pan a shake to coat the kernels with the oil. When the corn has popped and there are no more sounds of popping, remove from the heat and put the popcorn in a large bowl.

Pour the butter over the popcorn, sprinkle with the Parmesan and seasoning, then toss with your hands to coat the popcorn evenly. Taste, adding salt if desired.

Serve hot.

Charlie's Guacamole

My son Charlie is a terrific cook. He's also my biggest critic. I got tired of him telling me how to improve my food, so I finally turned guacamole duty over to him. He means business with this recipe and is much more precise than I am, so enjoy this simple yet perfectly balanced guacamole.

GF | DF | VG | V | Q! | MA

Prep: 10 minutes
Makes 4 servings

2 ripe avocados, pitted and peeled

Kosher salt

3 teaspoons fresh lime juice

2 tablespoons minced red onion

2 tablespoons chopped fresh cilantro

1 cup (145 g) raw corn kernels (optional)

Corn chips, jicama spears, and cucumber spears, for serving

Place the flesh of the avocados in a wide, shallow bowl with 1 teaspoon salt. (The salt is a great abrasive and makes it easier to mash the avocado.) Using a fork, pastry blender, or a potato masher, mash the avocados until smooth or to your liking. Stir in 1 or 2 teaspoons of the lime juice to start, then taste and add more lime juice and salt, if you like. Stir in the red onion, cilantro, and corn, if using.

Serve at once, with chips, jicama, and cucumber alongside, or cover with a layer of plastic wrap pressed onto the guacamole and store at room temperature for up to 2 hours before serving.

Buffalo Cauliflower Hot Wings

I love chicken wings—see Chipotle-Lime Wings (page 94) for proof!—but last year I decided on Super Bowl Sunday that what the world really needed was cauliflower hot wings. So, while all of my barbecue buddies were posting their wing recipes on Instagram, I decided to fill my feed with a step-by-step process of making these yummy snacks instead, and they were a total hit! If you're trying to eat more vegetables, promise me you'll try this once.

GF | *VG | V

Prep: 15 minutes

Cook: 30 minutes

Makes 4 servings

1 large head cauliflower (about 2½ pounds/1.2 kg), cored and cut into florets

¼ cup (60 ml) olive oil

1 teaspoon kosher salt

½ teaspoon freshly ground black pepper

1 teaspoon Italian Seasoning (page 62), optional

2 tablespoons unsalted butter or vegan butter

½ cup (120 ml) hot sauce, such as Frank's RedHot Original sauce

2 teaspoons honey or agave nectar

Carrot and celery sticks, for serving

Granch Dip (page 53), for dipping

Preheat the oven to 425°F (220°C). Line two baking sheets with parchment paper.

In a large bowl, drizzle the florets with the oil, then season with the salt, pepper, and Italian seasoning, if using. Toss to coat. Divide the florets between the baking sheets and spread into an even layer.

Roast for 15 minutes, then stir and continue roasting until very crispy on the outside, about 10 minutes longer.

In a small saucepan, melt the butter over medium heat. Add the hot sauce and honey and whisk to combine. Bring to a simmer, then remove from the heat.

Drizzle the sauce over the cauliflower, dividing it equally between the pans. Toss until evenly coated with the sauce. Bake for 5 more minutes.

Serve with celery, carrots, and Granch Dip on the side.

Scrumptious Salads

CHAPTER FOUR

I love salads, especially those that combine fruits, vegetables, and/or proteins. Every once in a while, I want greens to be the main event, but usually I'm looking for a quick way to assemble different ingredients that are really tasty while also doing something good for my health! The salads in this chapter do just that. The Every-Day Salad (page 106) is designed to be good enough to eat (almost) every day of your life! And the Little Gem Cobb with Green Goddess (page 103) and California Chicken Salad with Peanut Dressing (page 104) are good enough to be served for dinner or for impressing friends at lunch.

Little Gem Cobb with Green Goddess

Every time I see Cobb salad on a menu, I'm compelled to order it. Maybe that's because it's made with all my favorite ingredients, including bacon, avocado, blue cheese, and a creamy dressing. It's decadent for sure, but this version incorporates ingredients that are good for you, too. The Herby Green Goddess Dressing (page 58) is a better-for-you option than most store-bought dressings, which tend to be full of saturated fat, preservatives, and too much sodium. The trick to enjoying a Cobb salad whenever you'd like? Hard-boil some eggs when you meal-prep for the week, and make the dressing, too. Also, I like to cook a chicken once a week to make stock and shredded chicken, so I always have them at the ready.

GF

Prep: 15 minutes

Makes 2 to 4 servings

6 cups (330 g) shredded Little Gem lettuce (about 3 heads) or romaine lettuce

2 cups (390 g) shredded cooked chicken breast

1 cup (145 g) halved cherry tomatoes

1 ripe avocado, pitted, peeled, and diced

3 hard-boiled eggs, diced (see page 65)

½ cup (115 g) cooked, crumbled bacon (about 6 slices)

¼ cup (25 g) thinly sliced red onion (see page 65)

¼ cup (35 g) crumbled blue cheese or feta

Kosher salt and freshly ground black pepper

½ to ¾ cup (120 to 180 ml) Herby Green Goddess Dressing (page 58)

To serve family style, place the lettuce in one section on a serving platter. Continue adding the other ingredients to the platter in individual piles or rows. Sprinkle the vegetables lightly with salt and pepper. Serve the dressing on the side and allow people to help themselves.

Alternatively, put all the ingredients except the salt, pepper, and dressing in a large salad bowl. Sprinkle lightly with salt and pepper. Toss gently to combine, then add ½ cup (120 ml) dressing and toss gently with your hands. Taste, adding more dressing and salt and pepper if desired. Serve at once.

To store: Without the dressing, the salad can be stored in the fridge for up to 3 hours before serving. Simply dress the salad right before serving.

California Chicken Salad with Peanut Dressing

While I was visiting a friend in LA thirty years ago, she insisted we go look for movie stars at this new, hip place called the Cheesecake Factory in Beverly Hills. I don't know if I was more excited about the Chinese chicken salad I ate before my cheesecake or the fact we saw Brian Austin Green from *90210* sitting at the next table. The salad was beyond tasty but a far cry from healthy. With its crunchy wontons, sugary peanut dressing, and other sinful bites of goodness, it contains more than a day's worth of recommended fat and sodium and over 60 grams of sugar! Over the years, I've developed a better-for-you option without losing the amazing crunch, silky dressing, and delicious combination of cabbages, chicken, and fresh herbs. The rice paper crisps are fun and a family favorite, but you can certainly skip them and rely on the peanuts for crunch. This makes a terrific vegetarian or vegan salad if you leave out the chicken.

GF | DF | *VG | *V

Prep: 20 minutes

Cook: 10 minutes

Makes 4 to 6 servings

RICE PAPER CRISPS

Avocado oil, for frying

6 rice paper wrappers

CHOPPED SALAD

4 cups (280 g) thinly sliced napa (Chinese) cabbage

2 cups (190 g) thinly sliced red cabbage

2 cups (110 g) chopped romaine lettuce

2 cups (390 g) shredded cooked chicken (see Note)

¼ cup (13 g) fresh mint leaves, chopped

2 tablespoons fresh cilantro

1 carrot, peeled and shredded

½ cup (75 g) salted roasted peanuts

Black sesame seeds, for garnish

Peanut Dressing (page 57)

To make the crisps, in a large, heavy saucepan, heat 2 inches (5 cm) of oil over high heat to 350°F (175°C) on a deep-frying thermometer.

Break the rice paper wrappers into shards 2 to 3 inches (5 to 7.5 cm) wide. Using a wire skimmer, carefully lower a few of the shards into the oil, making sure they do not overlap. The rice paper will puff and crisp up immediately. Using the skimmer, transfer the shards to paper towels to drain. Repeat with the remaining rice paper shards.

To assemble the salad, put all the salad ingredients except the dressing in a large bowl. Toss gently with half of the dressing, then add more until the leaves are well coated and there is no dressing at the bottom of the bowl. Serve in individual bowls with a pile of rice paper crisps on top, then drizzle a little more dressing over each serving and sprinkle a few sesame seeds over the top.

To store: Without the dressing and toppings, the salad can be stored in the fridge for up to 4 hours before serving. Simply dress the salad and add the toppings right before serving.

The Every-Day Salad

Have you heard the story about Jennifer Aniston eating the same salad on the set of *Friends* every day for ten years? I have no idea if it's true, but the idea inspired me to make a salad that was so delicious, I'd want to eat it for lunch every day, too! The trick to being able to make a delicious salad any day of the week is to have a few key ingredients at the ready, so you don't have to cook them at lunch. When I get home from the grocery store each week, I make a Classic Shallot Vinaigrette (page 54), cook and shred some chicken, and toast some almonds or walnuts. Knowing I have the key ingredients on hand to make a delicious salad at any given moment is so calming as I move into my work week.

GF | V | Q!

Prep: 10 minutes

Makes 1 serving

4 cups (220 g) chopped romaine lettuce or mixed greens

½ cup (80 g) cored and diced red apple, such as Fuji

1 hard-boiled egg, diced (see page 65)

2 tablespoons chopped almonds or walnuts, toasted (see page 65)

2 tablespoons crumbled feta or goat cheese

2 tablespoons sliced green onions, including white and light green parts

2 tablespoons dried cherries or cranberries

2½ to 3 tablespoons Classic Shallot Vinaigrette (page 54)

Kosher salt and freshly ground black pepper (optional)

4 ounces (115 g) shredded cooked chicken, salmon, or shrimp (optional)

In a medium bowl, combine the lettuce, apple, egg, nuts, cheese, green onions, and dried cherries. Drizzle with 2 tablespoons of the vinaigrette. Toss to coat the leaves. Taste, adding salt and pepper, if desired, and a little of the remaining vinaigrette. Top the salad with chicken (if using) and drizzle with the remaining vinaigrette.

To store: Without the dressing, the salad can be stored in the refrigerator for up to 4 hours before serving. Simply dress the salad right before serving.

> TIP: HOW TO DRESS A SALAD PROPERLY
> The key to dressing a salad properly is to make sure that every leaf of lettuce or vegetable is lightly coated with dressing, without any of it remaining at the bottom of the bowl. So what's the trick? Add half of the dressing called for in a recipe to a salad bowl, then place the greens on top. Using your hands, gently toss the greens to ensure they are all well-coated. If more dressing is required, add a little bit at a time to continue to coat the leaves. If you accidentally overdo it and there is dressing at the bottom of the bowl, add some more greens to the mixture until all of the dressing is absorbed. Once the leaves are well-coated, taste a few, adding a sprinkling of salt to the salad if necessary, before serving.

Quinoa Salad with Chipotle-Lime Vinaigrette

When I discovered I was gluten intolerant ten years ago, my doctor told me I needed to "get on board with quinoa!" I did my homework and learned that it's actually a seed, not a grain. As a complete protein, high in healthful fats and fiber, and loaded with macro- and micronutrients, quinoa's health properties just won't quit! It's incredibly versatile, taking the place of couscous, orzo, and Israeli couscous in my recipes. I love that it absorbs the flavors of whatever I've added to it without getting soggy. Make sure you rinse it to remove some of the bitterness. The Chipotle-Lime Marinade is great used as a vinaigrette in this recipe, and you can add all kinds of delicious vegetables to make this salad your own.

GF | *DF | **VG | V | MA

Prep: 30 minutes

Cook: 25 minutes

Makes 8 to 10 servings

2 cups (340 g) organic white quinoa

Kosher salt

Two 15-ounce (430-g) cans black beans, drained and rinsed

1 cup (145 g) fresh or frozen corn kernels, defrosted (about 1 ear)

½ cup (30 g) sliced green onions, including white and light green parts

1 cup (4 ounces/115 g) crumbled cotija cheese (optional)

⅓ cup (17 g) chopped fresh mint

⅓ cup (15 g) chopped fresh cilantro

1 cup (145 g) cherry tomatoes, halved

½ cup (120 ml) Chipotle-Lime Marinade (page 59), plus more as needed

In a fine-mesh sieve, rinse the quinoa well under cold running water and drain. In a medium saucepan over high heat, bring 4 cups (960 ml) water and ½ teaspoon salt to a boil. Stir in the quinoa, cover, and turn the heat to medium-low. Simmer until the quinoa is tender and white "tails" (the seed's nutritious germ) are visible, about 18 minutes. Using a large spoon, transfer to a large bowl and set aside to cool to room temperature. Fluff with a fork to remove any lumps.

Add beans, corn, green onions, cheese, mint, cilantro, and tomatoes to the quinoa, along with ½ cup (120 ml) of the vinaigrette and a generous pinch of salt. Stir gently, then taste, adding more vinaigrette and salt if desired. Serve at once.

To store: Refrigerate in an airtight container in the refrigerator for up to 3 days.

Baby Kale Salad with Delicata Squash and Toasted Walnuts

In search of a quick lunch idea, I looked into my near-empty fridge and saw a sad bunch of lacinato kale staring back at me. In a moment of inspiration, I cut it into very thin slices (which is the best trick for softening it up a bit) and let it sit in some vinaigrette for a few minutes. I toasted some walnuts, shaved a little red onion on it, and tossed it all together. The flavor of the kale mellows out a little as it softens, and the contrast of toasted walnuts with a bit of the red onion was magical! Lacinato kale—also known as dino kale or cavolo nero—aids in digestion, metabolism, and bone and joint maintenance. To make this vegan or dairy-free, use Balsamic Vinaigrette (page 56) instead of the Lemon-Parmesan Vinaigrette.

GF | *DF | **VG | V | Q!

Prep: 20 minutes

Cook: 15 minutes

Makes 4 to 6 servings

2 bunches lacinato kale, stemmed (see Tip) and thinly sliced crosswise (about 4 cups/260 g)

½ to ¾ cup (120 to 180 ml) Lemon-Parmesan Vinaigrette (page 56)

1 pound (455 g) delicata squash, sliced into ¼-inch (6-mm) rings, seeded and skin on

1 tablespoon olive oil

Kosher salt and freshly ground black pepper

½ cup (60 g) chopped walnuts, toasted (see page 65)

¼ cup (25 g) thinly sliced red onion

TIP: To remove the kale from its stems, grab the bottom part of the stem on each leaf with one hand, then pull the leaves in the opposite direction with the other.

Preheat the oven to 400°F (205°C). Line a baking sheet with parchment paper.

Put the kale in a large salad bowl and add ½ cup (120 ml) of the vinaigrette. Using your hands, toss the kale thoroughly to coat it with the vinaigrette. Let the kale sit for 15 to 20 minutes to soften a bit.

Place the delicata squash rings on the baking sheet, brush both sides with the olive oil, and season with a generous pinch of salt and a grinding of pepper. Roast for 10 minutes, then turn with a metal spatula and roast another 3 to 5 minutes, or until they are barely cooked through and slightly browned on the edges.

Add the walnuts, red onion, and squash to the salad. Toss gently to combine, then taste, adding more vinaigrette or salt if desired. Serve immediately.

Watermelon, Cherry Tomato, and Jicama Salad with Mint

This crunchy salad of diced watermelon and jicama is easily transported to a picnic or backyard barbecue. For a more composed salad to serve at the table, slice the watermelon and jicama instead (see the variation). To make a vegan version of this salad, simply leave out the feta or use a crumbled vegan cheese.

GF | DF | ˙ˑVG | ˙ˑV | Q!

Prep: 20 to 30 minutes

Makes 6 to 8 servings

4 cups diced watermelon (1½ pounds/680 g)

1 pint (290 g) cherry tomatoes, halved

1 cup (130 g) diced jicama (6 ounces/170 g or about half a jicama)

⅓ cup (30 g) thinly sliced red onion

¼ cup (about 1 ounce/28 g) crumbled feta or goat cheese (see Note)

Kosher salt

2 tablespoons extra-virgin olive oil

1 teaspoon red wine vinegar or balsamic vinegar

2 tablespoons shredded fresh mint leaves (about 10 leaves)

Flaky salt, for finishing

In a large bowl, combine the watermelon, tomatoes, jicama, red onion, cheese, and a pinch of kosher salt in a large bowl. Drizzle with the olive oil and the vinegar. Stir gently with your hands. Sprinkle with the mint, then finish with a sprinkling of flaky salt.

VARIATION: To serve at the table, arrange all of the ingredients in a pattern on a serving plate, alternating slices of watermelon with slices of jicama. Sprinkle with the olive oil and vinegar, then with flaky salt. Serve at once.

Broccoli Slaw with Curry-Lime Vinaigrette

There is a broccoli salad sold at Whole Foods Market that I adore. The addition of candied cashews, bacon bits, currants, and loads of mayonnaise practically negate the health benefits of the broccoli, but when I'm really hungry, I just don't care. My goal with this recipe? To make a broccoli salad just as amazing but better for you. If you're looking to add more greens to your diet, put this recipe at the top of your "must try" list!

GF | DF | *VG | *V | Q! | MA

Prep: 10 minutes

Cook: 20 minutes

Makes 4 servings

2 tablespoons dried currants

¾ pound broccoli florets, each about ½ inch thick (12 mm) (about 6 cups/540 g)

2 tablespoons extra-virgin olive oil

Kosher salt

4 slices thick-cut bacon (about 2 ounces/55 g), diced (optional)

⅓ cup (30 g) thinly sliced red onion

3 to 4 tablespoons Curry-Lime Vinaigrette (page 57)

Preheat the oven to 425°F (220°C). Put the currants in a small, heatproof bowl and add boiling water to cover. Set aside for 10 minutes to rehydrate, then drain and set aside. Line two large baking sheets with parchment.

Spread the broccoli in a single layer on the prepared baking sheets and drizzle with the olive oil and ¼ teaspoon salt. Roast until the broccoli begins to caramelize around the edges but is still crunchy, about 7 minutes. Let cool on the pan, then transfer the broccoli to a medium bowl.

Meanwhile, if using bacon, in a medium skillet over medium-high heat, cook the bacon, stirring occasionally, until crispy, 5 to 8 minutes. Using a slotted spoon, transfer to paper towels to drain.

Soak the red onions in cold water for 5 minutes to remove the bite, then drain and pat dry with a paper towel.

Add the bacon (if using), red onion, currants, and 3 tablespoons of the curry vinaigrette to the broccoli and toss to combine. Taste, adding more salt or vinaigrette as desired. Serve right away.

To store: Refrigerate in an airtight container for up to 3 days.

Spring Farro Salad with Snap Peas, Asparagus, and Tarragon

There are two chefs who inspire me to make more interesting vegetarian dishes: Yotam Ottolenghi and Suzanne Goin. Every time I make one of their vegetable or grain dishes, I am blown away by their ability to bring out the flavor and texture of every ingredient. The magic is in treating each vegetable with love by caring for them when washing, slicing, and cooking them so that when they are combined, they sing. So, Yotam and Suzanne, this salad is for both of you.

GF | DF | VG | V | MA

Prep: 10 minutes

Cook: 40 minutes

Makes 4 to 6 servings

MUSTARD-GARLIC VINAIGRETTE

1 tablespoon coarse-grain mustard

1 clove garlic, minced

Kosher salt and freshly ground black pepper

¼ cup (60 ml) fresh lemon juice (about 2 lemons)

½ cup (120 ml) extra-virgin olive oil

———

1½ cups (300 g) farro, rinsed

Kosher salt

1 teaspoon olive oil

½ bunch asparagus, trimmed and cut on the diagonal into 1-inch (2.5-cm) pieces

1 teaspoon grated lemon zest

½ pound (225 g) snap peas, cut on the diagonal into 1-inch (2.5-cm) pieces

2 tablespoons pine nuts, toasted (see page 65)

2 tablespoons diagonally sliced green onions, including white and light green parts

1½ tablespoons finely chopped fresh tarragon, plus leaves for garnish

For the vinaigrette: In a medium bowl, combine the mustard, garlic, ½ teaspoon salt, and a few grindings of pepper. Whisk to combine. Add the lemon juice and whisk to incorporate. While whisking constantly, slowly add the olive oil. Taste, adding more salt if needed.

In a large saucepan, combine the farro, 4½ cups (1 l) water, and ½ teaspoon salt. Bring to a boil over high heat, then reduce the heat to low, cover, and simmer until the farro is fully cooked with a slight bite in the center, about 30 minutes. Drain the farro, then transfer to a large bowl. Drizzle half the vinaigrette over the warm farro and toss to coat evenly.

Heat a medium skillet over medium heat. Add ½ teaspoon olive oil, then add the asparagus, ½ teaspoon lemon zest, and a pinch of salt. Cook, stirring occasionally, until tender, about 5 minutes. Using a large spoon, transfer the asparagus to a plate to cool.

In the same skillet, repeat the process with the snap peas: Heat ½ teaspoon of olive oil, then add the snap peas, ½ teaspoon of lemon zest, and a pinch of salt. Cook, stirring occasionally, until tender, about 5 minutes. Using a large spoon, transfer the contents to a plate to cool.

Add the asparagus, snap peas, pine nuts, green onions, and 1½ tablespoons tarragon to the farro. Taste and add more vinaigrette and salt if desired. Garnish with the tarragon leaves, then serve at once.

To store: Refrigerate in an airtight container for up to 3 days. When ready to serve, refresh with a few tablespoons of the vinaigrette and add more salt if necessary.

Italian Orzo Salad

Orzo is a great choice for room-temperature salads and side dishes, and this spin on an Italian antipasti platter is a total hit! The orzo absorbs all of the delicious flavors of the vinaigrette and basil, and the veggies up the health benefits big time. To make this vegan, simply leave out the mozzarella.

GF | DF | *VG | V | MA

Prep: 15 minutes

Cook: 20 minutes

Makes 4 to 6 servings

RED WINE VINAIGRETTE

¼ cup (60 ml) extra-virgin olive oil

2 tablespoons red wine vinegar

Kosher salt and freshly ground black pepper

¼ teaspoon dried oregano

———————

Kosher salt

1¼ cups orzo (about 8 ounces/ 225 g)

1 teaspoon olive oil

1 clove garlic, minced

1 cup (115 g) diced zucchini

⅔ cup (3 ounces/85 g) mini mozzarella balls (ciliegine), halved

⅓ cup (3 ounces/85 g) cherry tomatoes, quartered

⅔ cup (100 g) diced jarred roasted red peppers

¼ cup (40 g) sliced pitted black olives

2 tablespoons thinly sliced fresh basil

For the vinaigrette: In a small bowl, whisk together the oil, vinegar, ½ teaspoon salt, a few grindings of pepper, and the oregano. Set aside.

Fill a large saucepan half full of salted water and bring to a boil over high heat. Add the orzo and cook, stirring occasionally, until al dente, about 8 minutes or according to the package instructions. Drain well and transfer to a large bowl. Add half the vinaigrette and toss to combine. Set aside to cool.

In a medium skillet, heat the oil over medium-high heat. Add the garlic and cook, stirring, until fragrant, about 30 seconds. Add the zucchini and cook, stirring occasionally until tender, about 5 minutes. Transfer the mixture to the bowl with the orzo and let cool.

To assemble the salad, add the mozzarella, tomatoes, red peppers, olives, basil, and the rest of the vinaigrette to the orzo. Taste, adding more salt if desired.

To store: Refrigerate in an airtight container for up to 5 days.

A Soothing Bowl of Soup

CHAPTER FIVE

I think there's a whole group of people in the world who think soup is the greatest invention of all time. For some reason, I know a lot of them! My readers are constantly asking me for more soup recipes. So, friends, here are my latest—and definitely greatest—submissions. In fact, French Onion–Mushroom Soup (page 123) and Chicken-Coconut Red Curry Soup (page 120) have become two of my favorite recipes ever.

Creamy Tomato-Mint Soup with Parmesan Crisps

Homemade tomato soup has little resemblance to the canned kind, which contains sugar and preservatives. I do love the addition of the Parmesan crisps and swirling cream into it for a little luxury, but you can certainly omit it from the recipe to keep it dairy-free or vegan. The fresh mint is a nice change from the more common addition of basil and works really well with the tomato, but feel free to use basil if you like.

GF | *DF | **VG | **V | MA

Prep: 20 minutes

Cook: 50 to 55 minutes

Makes 4 to 6 servings

3 tablespoons olive oil, plus more for garnish

½ yellow onion, diced

2 stalks celery, sliced

1 large carrot, diced

Kosher salt and freshly ground pepper

3 cloves garlic, minced

1 tablespoon tomato paste

1 teaspoon fennel seeds

3 cups (720 ml) chicken stock (page 43) or vegetable stock (page 44)

One 28-ounce (800-g) can crushed tomatoes

¼ cup (13 g) chopped fresh mint or basil, plus more for garnish

1 to 2 tablespoons fresh lemon juice (optional)

½ cup (120 ml) heavy cream (optional)

Grated Parmesan, for garnish (optional)

Parmesan Crisps (page 46)

In a large saucepan, heat the olive oil over medium heat. Add the onion, celery, carrot, 1 teaspoon salt, and a few grindings of pepper. Cook, stirring occasionally, until the onion is soft and translucent, 5 to 8 minutes. Stir in the garlic and cook until fragrant, about 30 seconds, then add the tomato paste and fennel seed. Cook until the tomato paste is brick red in color, about 1 minute.

Add a splash of stock to the saucepan and increase the heat to medium-high, stirring with a wooden spoon to scrape up any browned bits from the bottom of the pan. Add the remaining stock, the tomatoes, and the ¼ cup (13 g) mint and bring to a boil, then reduce the heat to low and simmer until the soup has thickened and the flavors have intensified, 20 to 30 minutes. Taste, adding 1 tablespoon lemon juice.

Working in batches, puree the soup in a blender (or use an immersion blender to puree it right in the saucepan). Pour the soup back in the saucepan and warm gently over low heat. Stir in the cream, if using. Taste, then season with salt, pepper, or more lemon juice as needed. Serve hot, garnished with a drizzle of olive oil and a sprinkle of mint and Parmesan if you like. Pass the Parmesan crisps alongside.

To store: Let cool completely. Refrigerate in an airtight container for up to 3 days or freeze for up to 3 months. To defrost the soup, place the container in a warm water bath until the soup loosens from the sides, then transfer to a large saucepan. Place over low heat, stirring frequently, until the soup thaws completely and is hot.

Chicken-Coconut Red Curry Soup

Kim Laidlaw, my editor for this book, suggested I add this soup to the master recipe list. Caitlin Charlton, my recipe tester, made her first batch of this for us to try, and I ate half of it for dinner! Using homemade chicken stock (page 43) makes a huge difference in this and other recipes, but there are certainly plenty of organic and tasty packaged stocks on the market as well. If you're in a soup rut, this is the recipe that will get you out of it!

GF | DF | MA

Prep: 30 minutes

Cook: 25 to 35 minutes

Makes 4 to 6 servings

1 tablespoon olive oil

1 red onion, diced

2 large carrots, peeled and diced

1 red bell pepper, seeded and diced

Kosher salt

3 cloves garlic, minced

1 teaspoon peeled and grated fresh ginger

1 tablespoon red curry paste

4 cups (960 ml) chicken stock (page 43)

One 15-ounce (430-g) can coconut milk

1 tablespoon fish sauce

4 cups (80 g) baby spinach

2 cups shredded cooked chicken (about 10 ounces/280 g)

2 tablespoons fresh lime juice, plus 2 limes, cut into wedges for serving

2 tablespoons fresh cilantro leaves

In a Dutch oven or other heavy pot, heat the olive oil over medium heat. Add the onion, carrots, bell pepper, and a pinch of salt. Continue to cook, stirring occasionally, until the onion is softened, 5 to 8 minutes.

Add the garlic and ginger and stir until fragrant, about 30 seconds. Stir in the red curry paste until the vegetables are evenly coated.

Add the stock, coconut milk, and fish sauce, increase the heat to medium-high, and bring to a boil. Reduce the heat to low, partially cover, and simmer until the soup has thickened slightly and the flavors come together, 15 to 20 minutes.

Stir in the spinach, allowing it to wilt for a minute, then add the chicken and the lime juice. Simmer until the spinach has wilted and the soup is hot, about 5 minutes. Taste and adjust the seasoning.

Ladle the soup into bowls, garnish with cilantro, and serve with lime wedges alongside.

To store: Let cool completely. Refrigerate in an airtight container for up to 3 days or freeze for up to 3 months. To defrost the soup, place the container in a warm water bath until the soup loosens from the sides, then transfer to a large saucepan. Place over low heat, stirring often, until the soup thaws completely and is hot.

French Onion–Mushroom Soup

I love French onion soup, especially when the crunchy crouton on top is loaded with melted Gruyère. Adding mushrooms gives this soup even more heartiness and depth of flavor. Because there are so many onions to caramelize, it does require patience. You can shorten the time by covering the pan to let the onions sweat. Uncover the pan to let the caramelizing begin, and don't stop stirring until they're deep brown in color. To make this vegan, choose vegetable stock and top the soup with the toasted bread, omitting the cheese.

GF | DF | *VG | *V | MA

Prep: 20 minutes

Cook: 1½ to 2 hours

Makes 8 to 10 servings

3 tablespoons olive oil

3½ pounds (1.6 kg) yellow onions, thinly sliced (about 5 onions)

Kosher salt

2 cups (½ pound/225 g) sliced cremini mushrooms

2 cups (½ pound/225 g) sliced king trumpet mushrooms

4 cloves garlic, minced

1 teaspoon minced fresh thyme

2 tablespoons dry sherry

8 cups (2 l) beef stock, chicken stock (page 43), or vegetable stock (page 44)

1 tablespoon fresh lemon juice

CHEESE TOASTS

8 slices sourdough bread or French baguette

1 tablespoon olive oil

Kosher salt

1 cup (4 ounces/115 g) shredded Gruyère cheese, plus more for serving

In a Dutch oven or heavy pot, heat 2 tablespoons of the olive oil over medium heat. Add the onions and 1 tablespoon salt, cover, and cook for 15 minutes, stirring every 5 minutes so the onions don't burn. Once the onions soften, reduce the heat to medium-low and continue to cook, stirring often, until the onions are caramelized to a deep golden brown, 45 to 60 minutes.

While the onions are cooking, place a large sauté pan over medium-high heat, add the remaining 1 tablespoon olive oil, and heat until the oil is smoking. Add the mushrooms and a generous pinch of salt. Let the mushrooms cook, without stirring, until they are browned and no longer stick to the bottom of the pan, about 3 minutes. Cook, stirring frequently, until the mushrooms are slightly softened, 8 to 10 minutes. Remove the pan from the heat.

Increase the heat of the onions to high and add the garlic and thyme. Cook until the garlic is fragrant, about 30 seconds. Add the sherry, bring it to a simmer, and stir with a wooden spoon to scrape up any browned bits from the bottom of the pot. Add the stock to the pot and bring to a boil. Stir in the mushrooms. Reduce the heat to low and cover partially. Simmer until the soup has thickened and the flavors have melded, 25 to 30 minutes. Taste, adding salt and lemon juice if desired to balance the sweetness of the onions.

While the soup simmers, make the toasts: Preheat the oven to 425°F (220°C). Line a baking sheet with parchment paper. Arrange the bread slices on the baking sheet in a single layer. Brush both sides of each slice with the olive oil and sprinkle with a little salt. Bake until the edges brown, about 7 minutes. Remove from the oven and top each slice with 1 tablespoon cheese. Bake until the cheese has melted, 1 to 2 minutes. Serve the soup hot, topped with the cheese toasts and more cheese.

The Best Meaty Chili

Elizabeth Taylor loved the chili served at Chasen's in Hollywood so much that she had it shipped to her on set in Rome when she was filming *Cleopatra* in 1963. The original recipe calls for a combination of ground beef and pork, which really does make a difference. The well-seasoned meat is combined with a rich, tomatoey base, beans, onions, and peppers. Instead of asking you to cook the beans from scratch, my version uses canned pinto beans, which will speed up the cooking time significantly without sacrificing much flavor. I also opt for olive oil instead of the original ½ cup (115 g) butter (can you imagine!), which adds plenty of flavor. Consider making a double batch and freezing half of this chili so you've always got a great meal at the ready.

GF | DF | MA

Prep: 15 minutes

Cook: 30 minutes

Makes 8 to 10 servings

3 tablespoons olive oil

1 red onion, diced

2 red or yellow bell peppers, seeded and diced

Kosher salt

3 cloves garlic, minced

¼ cup (13 g) chopped fresh flat-leaf parsley

1 pound (455 g) ground beef, preferably grass-fed

1 pound (455 g) ground pork

3 tablespoons chili powder

1 teaspoon ground cumin

One 28-ounce (800-g) can crushed tomatoes

Two 15-ounce (430-g) cans pinto beans, drained and rinsed

1 cup (240 ml) chicken stock (page 43), vegetable stock (page 44), or water

Shredded Cheddar cheese, sour cream, and/or sliced green onions for garnish

In a large Dutch oven or other heavy pot, heat 2 tablespoons of the olive oil over medium heat. Add the onion, bell peppers, and 1 teaspoon salt and cook, stirring frequently, until the onions have softened, 5 to 8 minutes. Stir in the garlic and parsley and cook until the garlic is fragrant but not burned, about 30 seconds. Transfer the onion mixture to a bowl.

Return the pot to medium heat and add the remaining 1 tablespoon olive oil. Add the ground beef and pork and cook, stirring constantly and breaking the meat up with a wooden spatula or potato masher so the meat is crumbly. Cook until the meat is barely cooked through, 5 to 8 minutes. Stir in the chili powder, cumin, and 1 teaspoon salt. Add the reserved onion mixture to the pot. Stir in the tomatoes, beans, and stock.

Bring the mixture to a boil over medium-high heat, then reduce the heat to low, cover partially, and simmer until the chili has thickened slightly and the flavors have melded, about 20 minutes. Taste and adjust the seasoning.

Serve hot in bowls with the toppings alongside for everyone to add what they like.

To store: Let cool completely. Refrigerate in an airtight container for up to 3 days or freeze for up to 3 months. To defrost the soup, place the container in a warm water bath until the soup loosens from the sides, then transfer to a large saucepan. Place over low heat, stirring frequently, until the soup thaws completely and is hot.

Tortilla Soup

It's no wonder chicken soup is considered a healing dish in many cultures—it's a cinch to make and full of ingredients that can help ward off colds, fight congestion, and boost immunity. (Thank you garlic, tomatoes, lime juice, and cilantro!) This one freezes incredibly well, so if your family loves it as much as mine does, make a double batch of the base and freeze half of it. Any time you're in a pinch on a weeknight, you can heat up the soup and serve it with diced avocado and shredded cheese alongside for people to add as they like.

GF | DF | MA

Prep: 15 minutes
Cook: 35 to 40 minutes
Makes 6 to 8 servings

1 ancho chile

1 tablespoon olive oil

½ yellow onion, diced

Kosher salt

3 cloves garlic, minced

One 28-ounce (800-g) can fire-roasted tomatoes

8 cups (2 l) chicken stock (page 43) or vegetable stock (page 44)

2 tablespoons fresh lime juice

2 cups (390 g) shredded cooked chicken

2 tablespoons chopped fresh cilantro leaves

TOPPINGS

1 or 2 avocados, pitted, peeled, and diced

Shredded Monterey Jack cheese

Tortilla chips

Lime wedges, for squeezing

Put the ancho chile in a small bowl and cover with hot water. Cover the bowl with aluminum foil and steep until soft, 5 to 10 minutes. Drain, discard the stem and seeds, and transfer the chile flesh to a blender.

In a large Dutch oven or other heavy pot, heat the olive oil over medium heat and add the onion and a pinch of salt. Cook, stirring, until the onion softens, 5 to 8 minutes. Add the garlic and cook until fragrant, about 30 seconds. Remove from the heat and let cool, then transfer to the blender with the chile. Add the tomatoes and 1 teaspoon salt and puree until smooth.

Pour the pureed mixture back into the pot and place over medium-high heat. Add the stock and 1 tablespoon of the lime juice. Bring to a boil, then reduce the heat to low. Simmer, covered partially, until the soup has thickened slightly and the flavors have melded, 20 to 25 minutes. Stir in the chicken and simmer for 5 more minutes. Stir in the cilantro. Taste and season with salt and the remaining 1 tablespoon lime juice, if desired.

Serve hot in bowls, with the avocado, cheese, and chips. Pass the lime wedges alongside.

To store: Let cool completely. Refrigerate (without the toppings) in an airtight container for up to 3 days or freeze for up to 3 months. To defrost the soup, place the container in a warm water bath until the soup loosens from the sides, then transfer to a large saucepan. Place over low heat, stirring frequently, until the soup thaws completely and is hot.

Vegetarian Black Bean and Chile Chili

This vegetarian chili, which is rich with the flavors of spices and peppers, takes full advantage of the amazing health benefits of dried beans. For a thicker texture to the chili, blend some of the beans to a smooth puree and stir it into the pot.

GF | DF | *VG | V | MA

Prep: 15 minutes, plus 4 hours to overnight for soaking

Cook: 1½ to 2 hours

Makes 6 to 8 servings

2 cups (370 g) dried black beans

3 tablespoons olive oil

1 red onion, diced

1 jalapeño, seeded and diced

2 cloves garlic, minced

1 tablespoon chili powder

1 teaspoon ground cumin

½ teaspoon dried oregano

¼ cup (60 ml) fresh lime juice

2 tablespoons minced chipotle in adobo

Kosher salt

TOPPINGS (OPTIONAL)

Thinly sliced cabbage

Thinly sliced fresh radishes

Cotija cheese, crumbled

Chopped fresh cilantro

Pickled Onions (page 46)

Lime wedges

Rinse the beans and pick them over for any rocks or debris. Put the beans in a Dutch oven or other heavy pot and cover with 2 inches (5 cm) of cold water. Let soak for at least 4 hours or up to overnight (or use my quick-soaking method on page 65). Drain in a fine-mesh sieve, then set aside.

In a Dutch oven or other heavy pot, heat the oil over medium heat and add the onion and jalapeno. Cook, stirring occasionally, until the onion is soft, 5 to 7 minutes. Add the garlic and cook until fragrant, about 1 minute. Add the chili powder, cumin, and oregano and cook, stirring, until fragrant, about 1 minute. Stir in the drained beans, 2 quarts (2 l) water, the lime juice, and the chipotle in adobo. Bring to a simmer, cover partially, and cook until the beans are just tender, 1 to 1½ hours depending on the age of the beans. Add 1 teaspoon salt. Taste and adjust the seasoning, if desired.

For a creamier soup, blend about half of the beans to a puree and return to the pot.

Serve in bowls with whatever toppings you like.

To store: Let cool completely. Refrigerate in an airtight container for up to 3 days or freeze for up to 3 months. To defrost the soup, place the container in a warm water bath until the soup loosens from the sides, then transfer to a large saucepan. Place over low heat, stirring frequently, until the soup thaws completely and is hot.

Hearty Minestrone with Meatballs

Minestrone is rich with ingredients that are good for you yet full of flavor, and almost any vegetable works well in this hearty soup. I love parsnips and carrots, but you can use celery root or diced Yukon Gold potatoes as well. Just use your favorite vegetables and get cooking! This recipe makes a large batch of soup; leftovers can be refrigerated or frozen.

GF | MA

Prep: 20 minutes
Cook: 40 to 50 minutes
Makes 8 to 10 servings

3 tablespoons olive oil

1 cup (110 g) diced red onion

1 cup (140 g) diced peeled carrot

2 small parsnips, peeled and diced

3 stalks celery, sliced

Kosher salt

3 cloves garlic, minced

1 tablespoon tomato paste

1 tablespoon Italian Seasoning (page 62)

6 cups (1.4 l) chicken stock (page 43)

One 28-ounce (800-g) can crushed tomatoes

One 15-ounce (430-g) can cannellini beans or garbanzo beans, drained and rinsed

4 cups (80 g) baby spinach

MEATBALLS

1 pound (455 g) ground pork or dark meat turkey

⅓ cup (30 g) freshly grated Parmesan cheese, plus more for serving

1 large egg, beaten

1 teaspoon minced fresh thyme

1 teaspoon Italian Seasoning (page 62)

Kosher salt and freshly ground black pepper

In a Dutch oven or other heavy pot, heat the olive oil over medium heat. Add the onion, carrot, celery, parsnips, and 1 teaspoon salt. Cook, stirring, until the vegetables have softened and the onion is translucent, 5 to 8 minutes. Stir in the garlic and tomato paste. Cook until the garlic is fragrant, 1 to 2 minutes.

Add the Italian seasoning, then add the stock and tomatoes. Increase the heat to medium-high and bring the soup to a boil, then reduce the heat to low, partially cover, and let simmer for 15 to 20 minutes. Stir in the beans and cook for 5 minutes longer.

While the soup cooks, make the meatballs: In a medium bowl, combine the meat, Parmesan, egg, thyme, Italian seasoning, 1 teaspoon salt, and ¼ teaspoon pepper. Stir until well blended.

Reduce the heat to low so that the soup is barely simmering. Using a small ice cream scoop or spoon, scoop up about 2 tablespoons of the meat mixture and form meatballs about 2 inches (5 cm) in diameter. Drop the meatballs gently into the soup. If the meatballs are not submerged, use a spoon to gently push them under so they can cook evenly.

Simmer until the meatballs are cooked through, about 10 minutes. Turn off the heat, then stir in the spinach and allow the leaves to wilt, about 5 minutes. Taste the soup and season with more salt or pepper if desired. Serve the soup hot, with Parmesan sprinkled on top.

To store: Let cool completely. Refrigerate in an airtight container for up to 3 days or freeze for up to 3 months. To defrost the soup, place the container in a warm water bath until the soup loosens from the sides, then transfer to a large saucepan. Place over low heat, stirring frequently, until the soup thaws completely and is hot.

Big, Bold Veggies

CHAPTER SIX

I'd like a blue ribbon that says, "Most Improved Veggie Cook." Writing this book helped me to come up with vegetable-centric recipes that are so good, you can serve them as the main event. If you already live a life full of veggies, I hope you'll find some new inspiration in this chapter to change up your daily routine. The Sheet-Pan Ratatouille (page 146) is one of the easiest, most delicious vegetable recipes of all time, and the Roasted Delicata Squash with Pomegranate and Pistachio Relish (page 132) takes the cake for the most beautiful vegetable recipe. (It also tastes as good as it looks!) Looking for a simple crowd pleaser? My Lemony Green Beans with Toasted Almonds (page 138) are always consumed down to the last bean.

Roasted Delicata Squash with Pomegranate and Pistachio Relish

Butternut squash might be most people's go-to, but it can be difficult and time-consuming to prep. Delicata is beautifully striped and easily sliced into rings. The rind is edible, so it doesn't even need to be peeled. The pomegranate and pistachio relish makes more than you'll need for this dish, but it is so versatile, it's worth it to make more. It can be piled onto any type of squash like kabocha or red kuri, spooned over roasted carrots (see page 142) or blanched green beans, and even used as a condiment with grilled chicken or fish.

GF | DF | VG | V | Q! | MA

Prep: 10 minutes

Cook: 20 minutes

Makes 4 servings

1 delicata squash (about ¾ pound/340 g)

1 tablespoon olive oil

2 teaspoons fennel seeds

½ teaspoon ground cumin

Grated zest of 1 lime

Kosher salt

———

POMEGRANATE AND PISTACHIO RELISH

⅓ cup (75 ml) extra-virgin olive oil

½ cup (75 g) pomegranate seeds

½ cup (60 g) chopped salted pistachios

¼ cup (13 g) chopped fresh mint

¼ cup (13 g) chopped fresh flat-leaf parsley

Juice of 1 lime

Kosher salt

Preheat the oven to 425°F (220°C). Line a baking sheet with parchment paper.

Cut the squash in half lengthwise. Use a tablespoon to dig out and discard the pulp and seeds. Cut the squash crosswise into ½-inch- (12-mm-) thick half-moons.

In a large bowl, combine the olive oil, fennel seeds, cumin, lime zest, and a pinch of salt. Add the squash and toss to coat. Spread the rings in an even layer on the baking sheet about 1 inch (2.5 cm) apart. Roast until the squash is tender, turning the rings halfway through cooking, 18 to 20 minutes. Remove from the oven and let cool slightly before arranging on a serving platter.

While the squash is roasting, make the relish: In a small bowl, combine the olive oil, pomegranate seeds, pistachios, mint, parsley, lime juice, and 1 teaspoon salt. Stir to combine, adding more seasoning or olive oil if desired.

Spoon a generous amount of relish over the squash and serve warm or at room temperature.

To store: Let cool completely. Refrigerate in an airtight container for up to 5 days. Let come to room temperature before serving.

Herb-Smothered Potatoes

Ina Garten is one of my favorite cookbook authors—her recipes are balanced, full of flavor, and they work every single time. It's impossible to choose my favorite of her recipes, but I especially love her technique of cooking potatoes in a covered pot. Ina uses plenty of butter and fresh herbs to season the potatoes, but olive oil works equally well (and makes for a better-for-you version). I shower mine with freshly grated Parmesan cheese for even more flavor, but you can leave it off for a vegan version. If you have leftover Classic Basil Pesto (page 51), replace the herbs and cheese with ½ cup (120 ml) of fresh pesto. It's heavenly!

GF | *DF | **VG | V

Prep: 10 minutes

Cook: 25 to 35 minutes

Makes 6 to 8 servings

¼ cup (60 ml) extra-virgin olive oil

3 pounds (1.4 kg) small white or Yukon Gold potatoes, scrubbed but not peeled

Kosher salt and freshly ground black pepper

1 garlic clove, grated

1 tablespoon chopped fresh chives

2 tablespoons chopped fresh flat-leaf parsley

2 tablespoons grated Parmesan cheese (see Note)

In a Dutch oven or other heavy pot, heat the olive oil over medium heat. Add the potatoes, 1 teaspoon salt, and ½ teaspoon pepper and stir to coat. Cover the pot with a tight-fitting lid, reduce the heat to low, and cook, shaking the covered pot every few minutes, until the potatoes are knife-tender, 20 to 30 minutes. (Shaking the pot prevents the potatoes from sticking to the bottom of the pot.)

Turn off the heat, add the garlic, and re-cover the pot. Cook for another 5 minutes. Toss with the herbs and Parmesan. Taste and adjust the seasoning. Serve hot.

VARIATION: Let the potatoes cool and refrigerate in a covered container for up to 3 days. Use a meat pounder or heavy pan to smash the cooked potatoes into ½-inch- (12-mm-) thick cakes. Place a large skillet over medium heat and add enough olive oil to coat the bottom of the pan. Cook the potatoes in batches until crispy, 2 to 3 minutes per side. Sprinkle with salt and enjoy!

To store: Let cool completely. Refrigerate in an airtight container for up to 5 days. To reheat, add the potatoes and 1 tablespoon water to a saucepan over medium heat. Cover and cook, stirring once or twice, until reheated, 5 to 8 minutes.

Amanda's Mashed Potatoes

Thanksgiving is my Super Bowl. I become a wild control freak, working off my calendar where I've timed everything out into 15-minute increments. While the turkey rests and the stuffing finishes in the oven, I make the mashed potatoes so they arrive at the table piping hot. Every single time, they're gone in minutes! My traditional recipe is loaded with cream and butter, but this better-for-you version is equally delicious. Using homemade chicken stock (page 43) instead of heavy cream or whole milk makes the potatoes silkier and a little fluffier. You can decide for yourself how much butter to add. For vegan mashed potatoes, use vegetable stock and vegan butter, such as Miyoko's Cultured Vegan Butter.

GF | *VG | *V

Prep: 30 minutes

Cook: 20 to 30 minutes

Makes 4 to 6 servings

3 pounds (1.4 kg) russet potatoes (about 6 potatoes), peeled and cut into 2-inch (5-cm) pieces

6 to 8 cups (1.4 to 2 l) chicken stock (page 43)

Kosher salt

4 to 8 tablespoons (55 to 115 g) unsalted butter

1 tablespoon chopped fresh chives, for garnish

> **TIP:** While you're peeling the potatoes, put the peeled ones in a bowl of cold water to release a little of the starch and to prevent them from turning brown.

In a large stockpot, combine the potatoes with enough chicken stock to cover them by 1 inch (2.5 cm). Bring to a boil over medium-high heat, 8 to 12 minutes. Reduce the heat to low and simmer gently until the potatoes are fork-tender, about 10 minutes more.

Place a colander over a large bowl and drain the potatoes, reserving the stock in the bowl. Transfer the potatoes to the pot and set the reserved stock aside.

Place the pot over low heat to cook off any excess liquid that remains, stirring the potatoes gently. Remove from the heat. Use a potato masher or ricer to mash them until they have reached the desired consistency (I go for lump-free). Stir in ½ cup (120 ml) of the reserved chicken stock and 2 teaspoons salt. Let sit for a minute to allow the stock to be absorbed before adding up to ½ cup (120 ml) more stock to reach the desired fluffiness. Add 4 tablespoons (55 g) butter and stir gently until melted. Taste, adding up to 2 more teaspoons salt if necessary. Add the remaining 4 tablespoons (55 g) butter if desired, or serve in a bowl with a few tablespoons of butter on top. Sprinkle with the chives and serve.

To store: Let cool completely. Refrigerate in an airtight container for up to 5 days. To reheat, add the potatoes and 1 tablespoon stock or water to a saucepan over low heat. Cover and cook, stirring once or twice, until reheated, 3 to 5 minutes.

Mashed Sweet Potatoes with Spiced Maple Butter

It's no wonder sweet potatoes are all the rage these days. With 400 percent of the vitamin A you need daily packed into one sweet potato, they're also loaded with other vitamins and minerals to help strengthen your immune system. I love grilling them in their skins or roasting them whole in the oven, drizzled with Chimichurri (page 49) or Romesco (page 50). But for a holiday feast, my favorite way to serve them is mashed with maple-sweet butter and fragrant spices. Unlike russets, sweet potatoes don't become glutinous or starchy with over-mashing, so they reheat well, too.

GF | V | MA

Prep: 15 minutes

Cook: 45 to 60 minutes

Makes 6 to 8 servings

3 pounds (1.4 kg) garnet sweet potatoes (about 6)

4 tablespoons (55 g) unsalted butter, at room temperature

¼ cup (60 ml) whole milk

1 tablespoon Autumn Spice Blend (page 64)

Grated zest of 1 orange

Kosher salt

3 to 4 tablespoons pure maple syrup

Preheat the oven to 400°F (205°C). Wash the sweet potatoes and prick the skins with a fork a few times. Place them on a parchment-lined baking sheet. Bake until the potatoes can be easily pierced with a knife, 45 to 60 minutes. Remove from the oven and let cool until they can be handled. Cut the sweet potatoes open and scoop out the flesh of each one, placing the flesh in bowl. Discard the skins.

Add the butter to the sweet potatoes and stir until melted. Using a potato masher or pastry blender, mash the sweet potatoes until smooth. Stir in the milk, then add the spice blend, orange zest, and 1 teaspoon salt. Stir in 2 tablespoons of the maple syrup. Taste, adding more salt or a little more maple syrup, if desired.

Serve in a bowl, drizzled with the remaining 2 tablespoons maple syrup.

To store: Let cool completely. Refrigerate in an airtight container for up to 5 days. To reheat, add the sweet potatoes and 1 tablespoon water to a saucepan over low heat. Cover and cook, stirring once or twice, until warmed through, 5 to 8 minutes.

Lemony Green Beans with Toasted Almonds

My family loves green beans. I used to think it was because I tossed them in butter, but that's not the case! It's simply about blanching them until they are bright green and crisp-tender. Loaded with vitamins A, C, and K, green beans are a great source of folic acid and calcium. I can't think of a better side dish that is also so good for you. If you want to make this for a crowd, this recipe easily doubles.

GF | DF | VG | V | Q!

Prep: 15 minutes

Cook: 13 to 16 minutes

Makes 4 to 6 servings

Kosher salt

1 pound (455 g) green beans, trimmed

2 tablespoons olive oil

¼ cup (30 g) slivered almonds

½ cup (60 g) thinly sliced shallots (about 3 shallots)

1 teaspoon finely grated lemon zest

1 tablespoon fresh lemon juice

1 tablespoon chopped fresh flat-leaf parsley

> TIP: Green beans can be blanched up to 1 day ahead. After cooling, drain, wrap in a clean dish towel, and store in a resealable storage bag or airtight container in the refrigerator.

Fill a large stockpot half full with heavily salted water and bring to a boil over high heat. Have ready a large bowl of ice water. Add half of the green beans to the water and cook until they are barely crisp-tender and bright green, 3 to 4 minutes. Using a wire-mesh skimmer, immediately transfer them to the ice bath to stop the cooking. Repeat with the remaining green beans. Drain well and set aside.

In a medium skillet, heat 1 tablespoon of the olive oil over medium heat. Add the almonds and a generous pinch of salt. Cook, stirring often, until the almonds are lightly toasted, about 2 minutes. Transfer to a plate to cool.

Wipe the pan clean, add the remaining 1 tablespoon olive oil, and place over medium-high heat. Add the shallots and another pinch of salt. Cook, stirring constantly, until softened and caramelized, 8 to 10 minutes. Add the green beans, toss with the shallots, and remove the pan from the heat. Add the almonds, lemon zest, lemon juice, and parsley. Taste, adding additional salt or another squeeze of lemon juice if you like. Serve immediately.

Roasted Cauliflower with Chimichurri

Roasted cauliflower with herbs and spices is one of my favorite dishes, and adding chimichurri makes it absolutely scrumptious. Not only is cauliflower packed with flavor, but it's full of fiber, B vitamins, and cancer-fighting antioxidants. Instead of almonds, you could add toasted pine nuts or omit the nuts altogether, but I do love the toastiness they add here.

GF | DF | VG | V

Prep: 20 minutes

Cook: 20 to 30 minutes

Makes 2 to 4 servings

2 tablespoons extra-virgin olive oil

2 teaspoons Italian Seasoning (page 62)

Kosher salt and freshly ground black pepper

1 head cauliflower (1 to 1½ pounds/ 455 to 680 g), cut into 2-inch (5-cm) florets

¼ cup (60 ml) Chimichurri (page 49), plus more for serving

3 tablespoons chopped salted, roasted almonds

Preheat the oven to 425°F (220°C). Line a baking sheet with parchment paper.

In a large bowl, combine the olive oil, Italian seasoning, 1 teaspoon salt, and a few grindings of pepper. Whisk to combine, then add the cauliflower. Using your hands, toss together until the cauliflower is evenly coated with the spice mixture. Spread the cauliflower into an even layer on the prepared baking sheet.

Roast, stirring once, until golden brown, slightly charred, and tender, 20 to 30 minutes.

Transfer to a serving platter, top with the chimichurri, and sprinkle with the almonds. Serve with additional chimichurri on the side.

To store: Let cool completely. Refrigerate in an airtight container for up to 2 days. Serve leftovers at room temperature (do not reheat).

Rainbow Carrots with Brown Butter, Honey, and Thyme

I have been lucky enough in my career to have met some of the best chefs around. I was a little nervous when I first met chef Ludo Lefebvre, as his TV persona can be intimidating. However, he and his wife, Krissy, turned out to be friendly and welcoming. My kids and I have enjoyed Ludo's LA bistro Petit Trois many times. Their steak frites is always a standout, but it was the carrots that had me mesmerized. I watched as the chef stood over a small copper saucepan, continually basting the beautiful small carrots with water and butter, then finished them with honey and some thyme. I went home and had to make my own (slightly easier!) version, an homage to that dish and an attempt to bring a little bit of Petit Trois into our home!

GF | V

Prep: 10 minutes

Cook: 25 minutes

Makes 2 to 4 servings

3 tablespoons unsalted butter

1 bunch small carrots (about 1 pound/455 g), preferably rainbow, peeled, thicker carrots halved lengthwise

Kosher salt and freshly ground black pepper

2 teaspoons honey

1 teaspoon finely chopped fresh thyme

In a large skillet, brown the butter over medium heat, swirling the pan frequently, until lightly golden brown and foamy, 3 to 5 minutes. Add the carrots, a generous pinch of salt, and a few grindings of pepper. Toss to coat the carrots in the butter. Add ¼ cup (60 ml) water and partially cover the pan. Cook the carrots for 7 to 10 minutes, or until they are knife-tender. Remove the lid and stir in the honey and thyme. Cook for another 5 to 10 minutes, or until the liquid has mostly evaporated and the carrots are glazed. Remove from the heat and serve hot.

To store: Let cool completely. Refrigerate in an airtight container for up to 5 days. Reheat in a skillet over low heat, stirring a few times.

Garlicky Roasted Broccoli with Cashews

I think I can get almost anyone to love broccoli and cauliflower. My trick? Roasting the florets at a very high temperature so they caramelize and become sweet and crispy, then dusting them with Parmesan straight out of the oven. (Of course, you can leave the Parm off to make this vegan or dairy-free.) To make the broccoli look a little more like a main event, I've chosen to keep the florets a little larger. However, the smaller you cut them the faster they cook, so it's entirely up to you.

GF | *DF | *VG | V

Prep: 5 minutes

Cook: 20 to 30 minutes

Makes 4 servings

2 pounds (910 g) broccoli florets (about 16 cups), each about 2 inches (5 cm)

3 tablespoons olive oil

Kosher salt and freshly ground black pepper

2 tablespoons chopped roasted cashews

2 cloves garlic, minced

Pinch of red pepper flakes

¼ cup (25 g) grated Parmesan (see Note)

Position two oven racks evenly in the oven and preheat to 400°F (205°C). Line two baking sheets with parchment paper.

Place the broccoli on the baking sheets, dividing them evenly between the pan and spacing them apart. Brush the broccoli on both sides with 2 tablespoons of the olive oil, and season both sides with salt and pepper.

In a small bowl, combine the cashews, garlic, and pepper flakes with the remaining 1 tablespoon olive oil. Set aside.

Roast the broccoli until it begins to brown around the edges, about 15 minutes. Remove from the oven and flip it, then pour the cashew mixture over the broccoli, dividing it equally among the pieces. Roast until the cashews are toasted and the broccoli is crisped a bit more, 5 to 8 minutes longer.

Sprinkle with the Parmesan cheese and serve at once.

To store: Let cool completely. Refrigerate in an airtight container for up to 5 days. Reheat in a skillet over medium heat, stirring often, until warmed through, about 5 minutes.

Warm Brussels Sprouts, Cabbage, and Apple "Slaw"

In the fall and winter, I crave braised food that is comforting, simple, and flavorful. Here, humble winter vegetables are transformed with a bit of lemon juice or a few drops of vinegar, along with a smattering of fresh herbs, which can make even the heartiest braises taste like spring. Chopping everything for this recipe by hand can take some time, so if you have a food processor with a slicing blade, use it to shred the cabbage and the Brussels sprouts in a matter of minutes. This recipe is so well-balanced—sweet and acidic, crunchy and fragrant—it's completely worth the extra effort. Serve this slaw with the Apple Cider–Brined Pork Chops (page 180), or with other veggie dishes for a vegetarian feast.

GF | DF | *VG | V

Prep: 30 to 40 minutes

Cook: 30 minutes

Makes 8 to 10 servings

4 tablespoons (60 ml) olive oil

1 yellow onion, halved and thinly sliced

Kosher salt

2 firm red apples, such as Fuji or Gala, halved, cored, and thinly sliced

2 teaspoons caraway seeds

1½ pounds (680 g) red cabbage, cored and finely shredded

1 pound (455 g) Brussels sprouts, trimmed and thinly sliced

2 tablespoons red wine vinegar

1 tablespoon Dijon mustard

1 tablespoon coarse mustard

Juice of 1 lemon (optional)

1 to 2 tablespoons honey (optional)

¼ cup (13 g) chopped fresh herbs, such as parsley, dill, or mint

In a large sauté pan, heat 2 tablespoons of the olive oil over medium-high heat. Add the onion and 1 teaspoon salt and cook, stirring frequently, until the onions have softened, about 8 minutes. Add the apples and caraway seeds and continue to cook, stirring, until the apples have softened, about 5 minutes.

Add the cabbage, Brussels sprouts, and 1 teaspoon salt. Stir to mix all the ingredients well. Add ½ cup (120 ml) water and bring the mixture to a simmer. Cover and reduce the heat to medium. Cook the vegetables, stirring every so often, until the cabbage and Brussels sprouts are crisp-tender, 8 to 10 minutes. Remove the lid and increase the heat to cook off any excess liquid, then reduce the heat to low.

Stir in the red wine vinegar, Dijon mustard, and coarse mustard to coat the vegetables. Taste and season with salt if needed. For a brighter finish to the vegetables, stir in the lemon juice, and if you'd prefer a little more sweetness, stir in the honey. Remove the braised vegetables from the heat and stir in the chopped herbs. Serve warm.

To store: Let cool completely. Refrigerate in an airtight container for up to 3 days. To reheat, add the slaw and 1 tablespoon water to a large saucepan over medium heat. Cook, stirring often, until warmed through, about 5 minutes. Taste, adding another squeeze of lemon or more fresh herbs if necessary to liven it up.

Sheet-Pan Ratatouille

As a kid, I really had a problem with zucchini. I remember it swimming around in its own water, with some canned cheese sprinkles on top. Clearly, I just needed a lesson on how to cook it. Once I experienced zucchini grilled, roasted, or shaved raw in salads, I fell in love with it. Then when I studied in France for a semester in college, I tasted the traditional Provençal dish ratatouille, the classic vegetable tomato-based "stew" of zucchini, eggplant, squash, and plenty of olive oil and garlic. Watching the movie *Ratatouille* recently reminded me how much I liked this dish, so I set out to make a version that wouldn't keep me in the kitchen for hours: sheet-pan ratatouille. This is a cinch to make, and roasting the vegetables coaxes out all of their flavors.

GF | DF | VG | V | Q! | MA

Prep: 5 minutes

Cook: 15 minutes

Makes 4 to 6 servings

1 zucchini, diced (about 2 cups/230 g)

2 Japanese eggplants, diced (about 2 cups/160 g)

¼ cup (30 g) thinly sliced shallots

2 cups (290 g) cherry tomatoes

4 cloves garlic, smashed

2 fresh thyme sprigs

3 tablespoons extra-virgin olive oil

Kosher salt and freshly ground black pepper

¼ cup (10 g) packed thinly sliced or torn fresh basil leaves

Position 2 oven racks evenly in the oven and preheat to 400°F (205°C). Line 2 baking sheets with parchment paper.

On one baking sheet, combine the zucchini, eggplants, and shallots. On the second baking sheet, combine the tomatoes, garlic, and thyme. Drizzle the vegetables on each pan with 1 tablespoon of the olive oil and sprinkle with a pinch *each* of salt and pepper, then toss to combine.

Roast the vegetables until the zucchini and eggplant are tender and the cherry tomatoes are bursting, 12 to 15 minutes, rotating the pans between the racks halfway through. Keep an eye on both pans, as one may need to be removed before the other.

Transfer all of the vegetables to a large bowl, discarding the thyme sprigs and garlic cloves. Stir in the basil. Taste, adding more salt if desired. Drizzle with the remaining 1 tablespoon olive oil and serve immediately.

To store: Let cool completely. Refrigerate in an airtight container for up to 5 days. To reheat, add the ratatouille and 1 teaspoon of water to a saucepan over low heat. Cook, stirring often, until warmed through, about 5 minutes. Drizzle with olive oil and sprinkle with salt before serving.

Spinach with Garlicky Bread Crumbs

Fast, tasty, and good for you, spinach is chock-full of vitamins A, C, K, folic acid, iron, and calcium. It also acts as an antioxidant to help boost your immune system while aiding hydration (it's practically all water), curbing your appetite, and when cooked, can help prevent bone loss. Spinach cooks faster than almost any other vegetable and makes a delicious backdrop for other flavors. For this better-for-you version, I added pine nuts and toasted bread crumbs for crunch and depth of flavor, plumped currants for a little sweetness, and lemon zest for a fresh hit of citrus.

*GF | DF | VG | V | Q!

Prep: 15 minutes

Cook: 5 minutes

Makes 2 to 4 servings

1 tablespoon dried currants

1 tablespoon extra-virgin olive oil, plus more for drizzling

Kosher salt

2 cloves garlic, crushed

1 pound (455 g) spinach leaves, washed and dried

2 tablespoons pine nuts, toasted (see page 65)

Grated zest of 1 lemon

1 to 2 teaspoons fresh lemon juice

1 cup (100 g) toasted fresh bread crumbs (see page 65), regular or gluten-free

Put the currants in a small bowl of hot water, cover, and allow them to rehydrate for 10 minutes. Drain and set aside.

In a large nonstick skillet over medium-high heat, warm the 1 tablespoon olive oil and the garlic cloves. Cook until fragrant but not burnt, about 30 seconds.

Add enough spinach to reach the top of the pan. Let wilt for 10 to 15 seconds without stirring, then add another few cups of spinach leaves to the pan. Using tongs, turn the spinach leaves, moving the wilted ones to the top and the raw ones to the bottom. Continue to add and cook the spinach, turning often, until the spinach has softened and given off some of its water, about 3 minutes. Keep the pan over the heat for about 30 seconds to let any excess water evaporate from the spinach.

Transfer the spinach to a serving bowl, sprinkle with a little salt, and let sit for a few minutes. Remove and discard the garlic cloves. If additional liquid collects in the bowl, drain it off before adding the other ingredients.

To serve, add the currants, pine nuts, lemon zest, and lemon juice. Stir gently to combine. Taste, adding more salt if needed. Drizzle with olive oil. Top with the toasted bread crumbs immediately before serving.

To store: Let cool completely. Refrigerate in an airtight container for up to 2 days. Store the bread crumbs separately.

Pot-of-Gold Cannellini Beans

When a friend asked me if I had a vegan bean recipe with all of the depth of flavor as my standard recipe, I panicked. But this version turned out so well that it's the only version I need now. Tomato paste replaced anchovies for the extra depth of flavor, and I subbed in a high-quality vegetable stock for chicken stock. (Of course, you can use chicken stock instead!)

GF | DF | VG | V | MA

Prep: 30 minutes, plus 1 hour to overnight for soaking

Cook: 3 to 4 hours

Makes 8 to 12 servings

1 pound (455 g) dried cannellini beans

4 cups (960 ml) vegetable stock (page 44) or chicken stock (page 43)

3 tablespoons extra-virgin olive oil, plus more for drizzling

1 red onion, diced

3 carrots, peeled and diced

Kosher salt

3 cloves garlic, minced

2 tablespoons tomato paste

1 tablespoon chopped fresh thyme

1 tablespoon chopped fresh rosemary

Juice of 1 lemon (optional)

Freshly ground black pepper

Flaky salt, for garnish

Soak the beans in cold water for at least 1 hour or up to overnight.

Drain the beans. In a large Dutch oven or other heavy pot, combine the beans, stock, and enough water to cover the beans by 2 inches (5 cm). Bring the beans to a boil over high heat, then reduce the heat to low until barely simmering. Cook, partially covered, stirring every so often, until the beans are tender to the bite, occasionally adding liquid as necessary to keep them covered, 1½ to 3 hours depending on the age of the beans. (Do not add any salt to the beans while cooking, or it will toughen the beans.) Drain the beans, reserving the cooking liquid. Wipe out the pot and place it back on the stove top.

Over medium heat, warm the 3 tablespoons olive oil, then add the onions, carrots, and 1 teaspoon salt. Cook, stirring, until the onions are soft, 5 to 8 minutes. Add the garlic, tomato paste, thyme, and rosemary and cook, stirring, until the garlic is fragrant, about 30 seconds.

Return the beans to the pot along with 1 to 2 cups (240 to 480 ml) of their cooking liquid (or water) so the mixture is the consistency of a thick chili. Simmer the beans over very low heat until the flavors meld and the liquid thickens enough to coat the back of a spoon, 20 to 30 minutes.

When the beans have reached the desired consistency, taste, adding the lemon juice if you like and season generously with salt and pepper. (Since the beans were not salted while cooking, you'll be surprised at how much salt they may need.) Turn off the heat and let sit for a few minutes to absorb the flavors.

Serve warm, drizzled with olive oil and a sprinkling of flaky salt.

To store: Let cool completely. Refrigerate in an airtight container for up to 3 days. To reheat, warm the beans and 1 to 2 tablespoons water in a large saucepan over medium-low heat.

It's All About Dinner

CHAPTER SEVEN

My family and friends had big opinions on what recipes should be featured in this book. They wanted new versions of my "greatest hits," like Connor's Macaroni and Cheese (which I can make in my sleep!) and Tex-Mex Skillet Casserole (page 175). They also wanted me to include the weeknight recipes that didn't make it into my last few books, like Orecchiette with Broccoli, Lemon Zest, and Parmesan (page 159) and Honey-Mustard Salmon (page 164). I sought to balance their requests with some of my favorite dinners that are full of better-for-you ingredients, like Braised Chicken and Bok Choy Rice Bowls (page 173) with a deeply flavored soy and sesame marinade. I also included my lowest-maintenance, make-ahead recipes for entertaining, like Citrusy Pulled Pork (page 183), served with Charlie's Guacamole (page 97). I hope you enjoy the most comprehensive dinner chapter I've ever written. I myself can't wait to cook from this chapter again and again.

Moroccan-Spiced Root Vegetables with Couscous

During college, I studied in France for a semester. It was the best decision I could have made. With no cell phone, credit card, or computer—does anyone even remember those days?—my time in France shaped me into the cook I am today. With only $800 for four months, I made sure that every week I could consume three chocolate croissants, imperial rolls at the best Vietnamese place, and lunch at my favorite Tunisian restaurant for couscous. That dish was an incredibly fragrant, brothy, spiced tomato stew of root vegetables served over a fluffy bed of couscous with chicken or merguez sausage on top. Thirty years later, I can still taste it. You can serve meat with this version if you'd like, of course, but it's absolutely delicious without it.

DF | VG | V | MA

Prep: 30 minutes

Cook: 50 to 55 minutes

Makes 4 to 6 servings

2 tablespoons olive oil

1 red onion, diced

Kosher salt

2 cloves garlic, minced

1 tablespoon curry powder

1½ teaspoons ground cumin

1 teaspoon ground turmeric

1 tablespoon tomato paste

2 parsnips, peeled and diced

1 turnip, peeled and diced

3 carrots, peeled and diced

2 cups (480 ml) chicken stock or vegetable stock (pages 43–44)

One 15-ounce (430-g) can crushed tomatoes

1 cinnamon stick

One 15-ounce (430-g) can garbanzo beans, drained and rinsed

1 cup (145 g) raisins

Cooked couscous, for serving

Chopped fresh parsley, for garnish

Harissa, for serving (optional)

In a large Dutch oven or other heavy pot, heat the oil over medium-high heat. Add the onion and 1 teaspoon salt and cook, stirring frequently, until the onion has softened, 5 to 8 minutes. Add the garlic and sauté until fragrant, about 30 seconds. Add the curry powder, cumin, turmeric, and tomato paste and cook, stirring, until the tomato paste has turned brick red in color, about 1 minute. Add the diced parsnips, turnip, and carrots and stir to coat them with the spices. Add the stock and crushed tomatoes and bring the vegetables to a simmer. Add the cinnamon stick, cover, and reduce the heat to low to simmer gently. Cook until the vegetables have softened and the flavors have melded, about 30 minutes. Stir in the garbanzo beans and raisins and let them sit in the broth for 10 minutes to plump before serving.

To serve, discard the cinnamon stick. Divide the couscous among bowls, then top with the vegetables and some of the broth. Sprinkle each serving with parsley. Serve with harissa alongside, if you like.

To store: Let cool completely. Refrigerate in an airtight container for up to 3 days.

Tofu and Broccoli Stir-Fry

I 'll admit, I don't naturally gravitate towards tofu. But every time I try it in restaurants, I love it! Its beautiful texture takes on bold flavors while still crisping on the outside, leaving you with pillowy bites of goodness with a crunch. My Asian pear marinade is the perfect foil for the tofu, but once you master the technique you can add any type of marinade you'd like!

GF | DF | VG | V | Q!

Prep: 15 minutes

Cook: 16 minutes

Makes 4 servings

15 ounces (430 g) firm or extra-firm tofu, drained and cubed

1 tablespoon cornstarch

2 to 3 tablespoons toasted sesame oil

Kosher salt

1 pound (455 g) broccoli florets (about 8 cups)

1 cup (240 ml) Sesame–Asian Pear Marinade (page 61)

Steamed rice, for serving (optional)

3 green onions, sliced, including white and light green parts, for garnish

Toasted sesame seeds, for garnish (optional)

Using paper towels, pat the tofu dry. Transfer to a bowl and add the cornstarch, then gently toss to coat.

In a large skillet, heat 2 tablespoons of the sesame oil over medium-high heat. Add the tofu and sear, flipping occasionally, until golden brown on all sides, about 10 minutes. If needed, add the remaining 1 tablespoon of sesame oil. Using a slotted spoon, transfer the tofu to paper towels to drain. Season the tofu with salt.

Add the broccoli to the pan and cook, stirring, until crisp-tender, about 6 minutes. Reduce the heat, then add the marinade and tofu to the pan and toss the ingredients together to coat completely.

Serve over rice, if desired, garnished with green onions and sesame seeds, if using.

To store: Let cool completely. Refrigerate in an airtight container for up to 3 days.

Lots-of-Veggie Fried Rice

I love rice. Especially white rice. I don't eat it very often, as it raises my blood sugar level, but sometimes it's the only thing I want to serve alongside a braised dish or a stir-fry. During the pandemic, I learned to always make extra rice, because my kids and their friends will eat it for days. So, I came up with a recipe for fried rice that has many redeeming health benefits, including being chock-full of veggies. You can add anything you like into this mashup, like leftover veggies, scrambled egg, steak, chicken, or tofu. Fried rice always tastes better when the rice is a day old because it gets crispy and browned, and adding a pinch of sugar while you're frying it is the secret to extra-crispy rice!

GF | DF | VG | V | Q!

Prep: 10 minutes

Cook: 15 minutes

Makes 4 servings

2 tablespoons olive oil

2 cups (280 g) finely diced mixed vegetables, such as carrots, broccoli, and celery

Kosher salt

⅓ cup (20 g) sliced green onions, including white and light green parts

3 cloves garlic, minced

3 cups (600 g) cooked jasmine rice, preferably 1 day old

½ teaspoon sugar

¼ cup (13 g) chopped fresh herbs, such as basil, mint, and parsley

In a large sauté pan or wok, heat 1 tablespoon of the oil over medium-high heat. Add the vegetables and a generous pinch of salt and cook, stirring constantly, until the vegetables are crisp-tender, 3 to 5 minutes. Transfer the vegetables to a bowl and wipe out any burnt pieces.

Return the pan to medium heat. Add the remaining 1 tablespoon of oil, then the green onions, garlic, and a pinch of salt. Cook, stirring constantly, until the garlic is fragrant, about 30 seconds. Add the rice to the pan, spreading it out and breaking it up with a metal spatula if needed. Sprinkle the sugar over the rice along with another pinch of salt and cook, letting the rice brown a little on the bottom before turning it. It's okay if the rice sticks to the pan a bit—that's the delicious part!

When the rice is crispy and cooked to your liking, remove from the heat and stir in the reserved vegetables and herbs. Taste, adding more salt if desired. Serve hot.

To store: Let cool completely. Refrigerate in an airtight container for up to 3 days.

Shrimp Tacos with Pineapple Salsa

We love tacos! I've got so many taco recipes circulating around the internet that I could write a taco cookbook. Meet my newest obsession, shrimp with pineapple salsa. These tacos are clean, bright, and crazy delicious! The fruit salsa is also delicious served with chips, spooned over grilled chicken, or served alongside other kinds of tacos.

GF | DF

Prep: 30 to 40 minutes

Cook: 5 minutes

Makes 4 servings

SLAW

4 cups (380 g) finely shredded green and/or red cabbage

1 tablespoon fresh lime juice

Kosher salt

PINEAPPLE SALSA

3 cups (495 g) diced fresh pineapple

½ cup (65 g) diced red onion

1 red bell pepper, seeded and diced (about 1 cup/145 g)

½ jalapeño, seeded and finely diced (optional)

¼ cup (10 g) finely chopped fresh cilantro

2 tablespoons fresh lime juice

Pinch of kosher salt

SHRIMP TACOS

1 pound (455 g) large shrimp, peeled and deveined

Taco Spice Rub (page 64)

1 to 2 tablespoons avocado oil

Eight 6-inch (15-cm) corn tortillas, warm

Charlie's Guacamole (page 97), Mexican crema or sour cream, and lime wedges for serving

To make the slaw, in a bowl, combine the cabbage, lime juice, and ¼ teaspoon salt and stir to combine. Let sit for 10 to 15 minutes to soften while you prepare the salsa and the tacos.

To make the pineapple salsa, in a medium bowl, combine all of the ingredients. Stir to combine then taste and adjust the seasoning.

To make the shrimp tacos, rinse the shrimp and pat it dry with a paper towel. Sprinkle the shrimp all over with the spice rub.

In a large nonstick skillet, heat 1 tablespoon of the avocado oil over medium-high heat. Add half the shrimp and cook, stirring frequently, until the shrimp are evenly pink and opaque, about 2 minutes. Using a slotted spoon, transfer the shrimp to a plate. Wipe the pan clean and repeat with the remaining oil and shrimp.

To assemble the tacos, place a few shrimp on each warmed tortilla, then top with the slaw, a generous spoonful of pineapple salsa, some guacamole, and crema. Serve immediately, with lime wedges alongside.

Penne with Eggplant, Tomatoes, and Smoked Mozzarella

My favorite Italian restaurant in San Francisco, Pane e Vino, closed during the pandemic. We used to live around the corner from it, and even after moving to the burbs almost twenty years ago, I'd still make an effort to eat there when in the city. Their fusilli con melanzane, or fusilli with eggplant, was transformative. Until I tasted it in 1995, I never understood the draw of eggplant and had never tasted smoked mozzarella. Together, they melt in your mouth. If someone in your house doesn't like eggplant, start here! Leave out the cheese to make a vegan version of this dish.

*GF | *DF | *VG | V

Prep: 20 minutes

Cook: 30 to 40 minutes

Makes 4 servings

4 tablespoons (60 ml) olive oil

1 red or yellow onion, diced

3 small Japanese or Chinese eggplants, trimmed and diced (about 3 cups/240 g)

Kosher salt

2 cloves garlic, minced

2 teaspoons Italian Seasoning (page 62)

One 28-ounce (800-g) can crushed tomatoes

3 tablespoons chopped fresh basil, plus more for finishing

12 ounces (340 g) regular or gluten-free penne or fusilli

¼ cup (25 g) Parmesan cheese, plus more for serving

4 ounces (115 g) smoked mozzarella, cut into ½-inch (12-mm) pieces

Bring a large saucepan of salted water to a boil over high heat.

Meanwhile, in a large skillet, heat 3 tablespoons of the olive oil over medium heat. Add the onion, eggplants, and 1 teaspoon salt and cook, stirring frequently until the vegetables have softened, 6 to 8 minutes. Add the garlic and Italian seasoning and cook until the garlic is fragrant, about 30 seconds. Add the tomatoes and bring to a simmer, then reduce the heat to low and simmer gently for 10 to 15 minutes. Taste, adding more salt if necessary. Stir in the 3 tablespoons basil.

Add the pasta to the boiling water and cook until al dente, about 8 minutes or according to the package directions. Drain the pasta, reserving 1 cup (240 ml) of the pasta water. Add the pasta to the sauce in the pan along with a splash of the pasta water and the Parmesan cheese. Stir until the pasta is well-coated in the sauce. Add the diced mozzarella and toss gently to combine. Remove from the heat. Taste and adjust the seasoning.

Serve at once, in pasta bowls, garnished with chopped basil and with Parmesan alongside.

To store: Let cool completely. Refrigerate in an airtight container for up to 3 days.

Orecchiette with Broccoli, Lemon Zest, and Parmesan

Why is orecchiette pasta so awesome? I'm convinced it's because the little ear shapes were specifically designed to catch bits of veggies or meat in them so that with every bite of pasta, you get all of the flavors in one place! When my kids were toddlers, this recipe was on repeat. They loved it, and I loved that they were consuming healthy amounts of broccoli, garlic, and olive oil. Simplicity never goes out of style, so this recipe had to go into this book. I hope it becomes your favorite go-to weeknight pasta recipe. To make this vegan, leave out the Parmesan or replace it with your favorite vegan cheese.

*GF | *DF | *VG | V | Q!

Prep: 10 minutes

Cook: 15 minutes

Makes 4 servings

12 ounces (340 g) regular or gluten-free orecchiette

2 tablespoons olive oil

2 cloves garlic, minced

1 pound (455 g) broccoli florets, finely chopped

⅛ teaspoon red pepper flakes

Kosher salt

Grated zest and juice of 1 lemon

½ cup (50 g) grated Parmesan cheese

Freshly ground black pepper

Bring a large saucepan of salted water to a boil over high heat. Add the pasta and cook until al dente, about 8 minutes or according to the package directions. Drain the pasta, reserving 1 cup (240 ml) of the pasta water.

While the pasta cooks, heat the olive oil in a large skillet over medium heat. Add the garlic and cook until fragrant, about 30 seconds. Add the broccoli, pepper flakes, and a generous pinch of salt and cook, stirring frequently, until well coated in the olive oil. Add 2 tablespoons of water to the pan and cover. Steam the broccoli until crisp-tender, about 2 minutes. Stir in the lemon zest and 1 tablespoon of lemon juice and remove from the heat.

Add the drained pasta to the broccoli mixture and place over medium heat. Add 1 tablespoon of the reserved pasta water along with half of the Parmesan and stir gently to coat. Taste, adding more salt, lemon juice, and a few grindings of black pepper, if desired. Divide among 4 pasta bowls, sprinkle with the remaining cheese, and serve.

To store: Let cool completely. Refrigerate in an airtight container for up to 3 days.

THE Lasagna

I used to spend hours making my mom's lasagna, cooking the sauce from scratch and boiling the noodles before baking, which was always a sticky mess! Then one day, pressed for time, I used no-boil gluten-free noodles (my favorite brand is Jovial no-bake gluten-free noodles) and jarred pasta sauce. Everyone raved at the results! This is now my go-to recipe. Jarred pasta sauces have come a long way—it's now easy to find organic, tomato-based pasta sauces that aren't loaded with sugar and cost only a few bucks. You can assemble the lasagna in the morning and keep it in the refrigerator until you're ready to bake it, or bake it over the weekend, then let people reheat it by the slice all week long. (We can't seem to keep a baked one in the fridge for more than a day or two!) I love the addition of a layer of Classic Basil Pesto (page 51).

*GF | V

Prep: 20 minutes

Cook: 55 to 75 minutes

Makes 8 to 12 servings

4 cups (1 pound/455 g) shredded mozzarella

¾ cup (75 g) grated Parmesan

15 ounces (430 g) whole-milk ricotta

Freshly ground black pepper

1 large egg, lightly beaten

Two (25-ounce/710g) jars tomato-basil or marinara sauce

1 package (12 noodles) no-bake lasagna noodles (regular or gluten-free)

½ cup (120 ml) pesto, homemade (page 51) or store-bought

Preheat the oven to 375°F (190°C).

In a small bowl, combine 1 cup (110 g) of the mozzarella and ¼ cup (25 g) of the Parmesan. Set aside to top the lasagna.

In a medium bowl, combine the remaining 3 cups (330 g) of mozzarella with the ricotta and remaining ½ cup (50 g) of Parmesan. Stir to combine. Taste, adding a few grindings of pepper if desired. Add the egg and stir to combine.

To assemble the lasagna, spread a few tablespoons of tomato sauce across the bottom of an 8 by 12-inch (20 by 30.5-cm) or 9 by 13-inch (23 by 33-cm) baking dish. Place 4 of the lasagna noodles crosswise in the pan, letting them overlap a bit if necessary. (If the noodles you are using cover the length of the pan, place 3 of the noodles lengthwise to create the first layer.)

Drop half of the ricotta cheese mixture in spoonfuls across the noodles. Spread it out evenly with a rubber spatula. Pour half of the pesto over the ricotta mixture and spread it out evenly with the spatula. Then spread one-third of the tomato sauce over to cover evenly.

Repeat with another layer of noodles, the remaining ricotta mixture, the remaining pesto, and one-third of the tomato sauce.

continued . . .

Add the final layer of noodles, then the remaining tomato sauce, ensuring the noodles are totally covered with the sauce. Sprinkle the reserved cheese mixture over the entire lasagna. Cover the pan tightly with aluminum foil and place on a baking sheet. Bake until the lasagna is bubbling hot and the noodles are tender, 50 to 60 minutes. To test, lift a corner of the foil and insert a paring knife into the lasagna; it should pierce the noodles easily. If the noodles are not done, cover and continue cooking for another 10 minutes. When cooked, remove the foil and bake for another 5 minutes, or until the cheese is golden brown.

Let the lasagna cool for 20 to 30 minutes before cutting it into squares and serving.

To store: Let cool completely, cover, and refrigerate for up to 3 days.

TIP: Because I tend to make lasagna once a week when my kids are home, I love varying it week to week to change things up! A few of my favorite additions are: adding 2 cups (240 g) cooked and crumbled Italian sausage to the tomato sauce; folding 2 cups (160 g) of finely diced, sautéed zucchini or eggplant into the tomato sauce; or replacing the mozzarella with smoked mozzarella for a smoky flavor that is out of this world!

Connor's Macaroni and Cheese

Every year on their birthdays, my sons get to request their favorite meal. But the tradition has gotten totally out of control. Now, they request breakfast, lunch, dinner, and a special homemade cake. My son Connor is an absolute creature of habit and he requests this mac 'n' cheese along with my Five-Star Five-Spice Ribs (page 181) every single year. Then he wants either a homemade apple pie or a three-layer lemon cake filled with lemon curd and frosted with vanilla buttercream. (Can we say lucky?)

*GF | V

Prep: 30 minutes

Cook: 40 minutes

Makes 6 to 8 servings

10 tablespoons (140 g) unsalted butter

Kosher salt and freshly ground black pepper

1 pound (455 g) regular or gluten-free macaroni or penne

3 cups (720 ml) whole milk

6 tablespoons (45 g) all-purpose flour or gluten-free flour blend, such as Bob's Red Mill 1-to-1 Baking Flour

3 cups (345 g) shredded mild or sharp Cheddar cheese

1 cup (80 g) panko (Japanese bread crumbs)

Preheat the oven to 350°F (175°C). Butter a 9 by 13-inch (23 by 33-cm) baking dish with 1 tablespoon of the butter.

Bring a large saucepan of salted water to a boil. Add the pasta and cook until al dente, about 8 minutes or according to the package directions. Drain the pasta and transfer to a large bowl.

Meanwhile, in a small saucepan over low heat, warm the milk. Remove from the heat.

In a medium saucepan, melt 6 tablespoons (85 g) of the butter over medium heat. Sprinkle the flour over the butter and whisk the mixture constantly for 2 minutes. (If the flour mixture starts to brown, immediately remove it from the heat.)

Gradually whisk in the warm milk, ½ cup (120 ml) at a time, until it is absorbed and there are no lumps. Cook, stirring, until the mixture thickens and begins to boil, about 5 minutes. Turn off the heat, add the cheese, and stir gently until the cheese melts and makes a smooth sauce. Taste, then season generously with salt and pepper. Pour the cheese sauce over the macaroni and stir gently to mix. Transfer the pasta to the prepared baking dish.

Melt the remaining 3 tablespoons of butter, then stir into the panko. Sprinkle the crumbs evenly over the pasta. Bake, uncovered, until golden brown and bubbly, 20 to 30 minutes. Serve hot!

To store: Let cool completely. Refrigerate in an airtight container for up to 3 days.

Honey-Mustard Salmon

Every time I try to fancy up this recipe, my family asks, "Why did you change it?" The two-ingredient glaze is great with salmon but equally good for chicken wings and roast chicken. Make sure to select salmon fillets of equal thickness so they cook evenly. Serve with Amanda's Mashed Potatoes (page 136) or Lemony Green Beans with Toasted Almonds (page 138).

GF | DF | Q!

Prep: 5 minutes

Cook: 10 minutes

Makes 4 servings

¼ cup (60 ml) Dijon mustard

¼ cup (60 ml) honey

Four 4-ounce (115-g) salmon fillets, pin bones removed

Kosher salt

Preheat the oven to 400°F (205°C). Line a baking sheet with parchment paper. In a small bowl, combine the Dijon mustard and honey.

Pat the salmon dry with a paper towel. Place the fish on the prepared pan skin-side down and sprinkle with 1 teaspoon salt. Bake until almost cooked through, 5 to 8 minutes. Remove the salmon from the oven and brush generously with the honey-mustard glaze. Return to the oven and roast until golden brown, about 2 minutes. Serve hot.

Grilled Whole Fish with Citrus-Garlic Sauce

Grilling whole fish is surprisingly easy. And fish cooked on the bone is much more flavorful than fish fillets. Just be sure your fish is fresh. It should have clear eyes and smell like the ocean. My favorite fish to roast whole are snapper, branzino, and trout. When purchased whole, the fishmonger should have already gutted and scaled the fish for you, leaving the bones in. Depending on the type of fish, they will vary in size from 1 to 2 pounds. For serving, plan on 1 pound of fish per person (the bones add quite a bit of weight).

GF | DF

Prep: 15 minutes

Cook: 25 to 30 minutes

Makes 4 servings

2 whole bone-in fish (about 2 pounds/ 910 g each), such as red snapper, branzino, or trout, gutted and scaled

Extra-virgin olive oil

Kosher salt

1 lemon, sliced into ¼-inch (6-mm) rounds

½ fennel bulb, cored and thinly sliced lengthwise

2 cloves garlic, thinly sliced

4 sprigs fresh flat-leaf parsley, plus chopped parsley for garnish

4 sprigs fresh mint, plus chopped mint for garnish

_____

CITRUS-GARLIC SAUCE

¼ cup (60 ml) extra-virgin olive oil

1 teaspoon finely grated lemon zest

1 tablespoon fresh lemon juice

2 tablespoons chopped fresh mint or flat-leaf parsley

3 tablespoons dried currants

1 tablespoon capers

2 cloves garlic, grated

Kosher salt and freshly ground black pepper

Preheat the oven to 400°F (205°C) or prepare a grill for direct cooking over medium-high heat (400°F/205°C).

Rinse the fish and pat it dry with paper towels inside and out. Lightly brush the outside and inside of the fish with oil, then sprinkle salt evenly over the inside of the fish. Layer the lemon slices, fennel, garlic, and 4 sprigs *each* parsley and mint evenly inside the fish. Place the oiled fish on a baking sheet if roasting or in a grill-proof roasting pan if grilling.

For the sauce: In a medium bowl, combine the olive oil, lemon zest and juice, mint, currants, capers, garlic, a pinch of salt, and a few grindings of pepper. Stir and set aside.

Place the baking sheet in the oven or the roasting pan on the grill and close the grill. Cook until the flesh flakes easily when poked with a fork, 20 to 30 minutes in the oven or 25 to 35 minutes on the grill.

Transfer the fish to a platter and let rest for 10 minutes. While the fish is resting, rewarm the sauce. Pour half of the sauce over the whole fish and garnish with the chopped parsley and mint. Serve, passing the remaining sauce at the table.

Sheet-Pan Halibut with Pesto and Spring Vegetables

Sheet-pan dinners are beloved by cooks these days, as they are both easy and simple. Here's one that's also rich with flavor. Any firm-fleshed fish will work here—salmon is a favorite in our house—but halibut cooks very quickly so it works especially well with this preparation. And while homemade pesto (page 51) is outstanding, don't be afraid to use store-bought in a pinch.

GF | Q!

Prep: 10 minutes

Cook: 10 minutes

Makes 4 servings

1 bunch medium-sized asparagus (about 1 pound/455 g)

Four 4-ounce (115-g) boneless halibut fillets, skinned

2 tablespoons olive oil

Kosher salt and freshly ground black pepper

1 cup (145 g) fresh corn kernels (about 2 ears)

1 cup (145 g) cherry tomatoes

Grated zest and juice of 1 lemon

½ cup (120 ml) pesto, homemade (page 51) or store-bought

Fresh basil leaves, for garnish

Preheat the oven to 400°F (205°C). Line a baking sheet with parchment paper.

Trim the woody ends of the asparagus spears by snapping off the bottom 2 inches (5 cm) or by using a vegetable peeler to peel the skin. Cut the asparagus diagonally into ½-inch (12-mm) pieces; you should have about 2 cups (270 g).

Pat the halibut dry with a paper towel. Brush both sides of the fish with 1 tablespoon of the oil, then sprinkle each piece generously with salt and pepper on both sides. Place the fillets on the prepared pan a few inches apart.

In a medium bowl, combine the asparagus, corn, and tomatoes. Drizzle with the remaining 1 tablespoon olive oil, ½ teaspoon salt, and a few grindings of pepper. Scatter the vegetables evenly around the fish on the baking sheet, making sure to leave some space between the ingredients so they can cook evenly. (If there are too many vegetables for one pan, place the remainder on another baking sheet and roast separately.)

Roast, stirring the vegetables halfway through the cooking time, until the halibut flakes with a fork but is not dry, 8 to 10 minutes.

Sprinkle the fish and vegetables with the lemon zest and a few teaspoons of the lemon juice. Drizzle with the pesto, garnish with the basil leaves, and serve immediately.

Sheet-Pan Spiced Chicken Thighs

I love creating a recipe and then finding ways to simplify it. This recipe started as a beautiful whole-roasted chicken with a chermoula sauce—a green sauce popular in Moroccan cuisine. Over time, it has evolved into a sheet-pan recipe, which reduces the prep and cook time by a solid 45 minutes. Instead of chermoula, I use Chimichurri (page 49), which is always on hand in my kitchen and super easy and quick to make. Feel free to substitute any root vegetables you like. This is my go-to combination.

GF | DF

Prep: 20 minutes

Cook: 30 minutes

Makes 4 to 6 servings

2 tablespoons olive oil

1 tablespoon Moroccan Spice Blend (page 63)

1 teaspoon kosher salt

6 boneless, skinless chicken thighs (about 2 pounds/910 g)

2 carrots, peeled and cut into 1-inch (2.5-cm) pieces

1 red onion, quartered

2 small parsnips, peeled and diced

Chimichurri (page 49), for serving

In a large bowl, combine the oil, spice blend, and salt. Add the chicken pieces, turning them to coat evenly. Set aside at room temperature for up to 1 hour or refrigerate for up to 4 hours. (If refrigerated, let stand at room temperature for 30 minutes before cooking.)

Preheat the oven to 400°F (205°C). Line two baking sheets with parchment paper.

Add the vegetables to the marinating chicken and stir to coat. Arrange the chicken and vegetables in an even layer on the baking sheets. Bake, stirring the vegetables once during cooking, until knife-tender, 25 to 30 minutes.

Let the chicken rest for 5 minutes before serving. Drizzle with chimichurri and serve more alongside.

To store: Let cool completely. Refrigerate in an airtight container for up to 3 days.

Skillet Chicken with Rosemary and Lemon

Roast chicken is a staple in my house. This one is cooked in a cast-iron skillet, an inexpensive and versatile pan that can also be used for frying and braising. Plus, the cast iron retains the heat well so when it is preheated in the oven, you'll get beautiful crispy skin and an even cook on the entire bird. A 10-inch (25-cm) pan works best so you don't get a bunch of burned bits on the exposed part of the pan. You can salt the chicken the night before to help dry out the skin and make it extra crispy. Or, if you don't have time, make sure to dry the skin well with paper towels. The Herb-Smothered Potatoes (page 135) are a great accompaniment to this chicken.

GF

Prep: 10 minutes

Cook: 50 to 70 minutes

Makes 4 servings

One whole chicken (about 4 pounds/1.8 kg)

2 tablespoons olive oil

Kosher salt

2 lemons, halved, plus juice of 1 lemon

3 sprigs fresh rosemary and/or thyme

3 tablespoons unsalted butter

Preheat the oven to 400°F (205°C) with a 10-inch (25-cm) cast-iron pan inside.

Rub the chicken all over with the olive oil, then season with 2 teaspoons salt, making sure to season the bottom and the body cavity. Stuff the body cavity of the chicken with the lemon halves and herb sprigs.

Carefully transfer the chicken to the hot cast-iron pan, breast side up. Bake until an instant-read thermometer registers 160°F (71°C) when inserted in the breast and not touching bone, or until the juices run clear when pierced with a knife, 50 to 70 minutes. If the skin starts to look overly brown, tent the bird with aluminum foil. Transfer the chicken to a cutting board and let rest for 15 minutes.

While the chicken rests, strain the juices through a fine-mesh sieve into a small saucepan, discarding any solids. Add the butter and warm over medium heat, whisking to combine. Taste, adding lemon juice and salt if needed.

Remove the herbs and lemons from the chicken cavity, then carve and assemble on a platter. Serve the pan juices alongside the chicken.

To store: Let cool completely. Refrigerate in an airtight container for up to 3 days.

Creamy Chicken Spaghetti with Lemon and Basil

"Can you make that creamy chicken pasta?" If I had a dollar for every time I heard that request, I'd be retired by now. Adults, neighbors, teens, and kids alike have been requesting this pasta from me for years. And I crave it, too! Instead of relying solely on heavy cream for flavor, I use some homemade chicken stock as well, which provides a silky texture and loads of flavor. If you don't have any on hand, pasta water can also be used to replace half of the cream. So many other ingredients can be added to this recipe. Sautéed mushrooms, leeks, or broccoli florets would all be delicious additions or fine substitutes for the chicken.

*GF

Prep: 15 minutes

Cook: 20 minutes

Makes 6 to 8 servings

12 ounces (340 g) regular or gluten-free spaghetti

2 tablespoons olive oil

1 large red onion, sliced lengthwise (about 2 cups/200 g)

Kosher salt

2 cloves garlic, minced

⅛ teaspoon red pepper flakes

2 cups shredded cooked chicken (about 1 pound/455 g)

½ cup (120 ml) chicken stock (page 43)

½ cup (50 g) grated Parmesan cheese, plus more for garnish

½ cup (120 ml) heavy cream

Grated zest and juice of 1 lemon

Freshly ground black pepper

¼ cup finely shredded basil, plus more for garnish

Bring a large saucepan of salted water to a boil over high heat. Add the pasta and cook until al dente, about 8 minutes or according to the package directions. Drain the pasta, reserving 1 cup (240 ml) of the pasta water.

While the pasta is cooking, in a medium skillet, heat the oil over medium heat. Add the onion and a generous pinch of salt. Cook, stirring frequently, until the onion is soft, 5 to 8 minutes. Add the garlic and pepper flakes and cook, stirring, until the garlic is fragrant, about 30 seconds.

Reduce the heat to low and stir in the shredded chicken. Add the drained pasta to the pan along with the chicken stock and Parmesan. Stir to coat, then add the cream, lemon zest and juice, 1 teaspoon salt, and a few grindings of pepper. Stir the pasta gently with tongs to incorporate the cream, adding a splash of pasta water to reach your desired thickness. Fold in the basil. Taste and adjust the seasoning with more lemon juice or salt, if desired.

Divide among pasta bowls, then garnish with additional Parmesan and basil. Serve at once.

To store: Let cool completely. Refrigerate in an airtight container for up to 3 days.

TIP: The pasta should finish cooking at the same time or right after the sauce is ready. If you drain it and let it sit around for too long, it will lose its beautiful texture, so when in doubt, cook it last!

Braised Chicken and Bok Choy Rice Bowls

After I fell in love with the Sesame–Asian Pear Marinade (page 61), I couldn't stop using it! Although it is absolutely delicious on the Tofu and Broccoli Stir-Fry (page 154), I love using it with chicken thighs and bok choy to create a hearty braise. I recommend making the marinade ahead of time so you can throw together a delicious, healthy meal any night of the week.

GF | DF

Prep: 15 minutes

Cook: 35 to 45 minutes

Makes 4 servings

4 chicken thighs (about 2 pounds/910 g)

1 cup (240 ml) Sesame–Asian Pear Marinade (page 61)

1 tablespoon toasted sesame oil

1½ cups (360 ml) chicken stock (page 43)

3 bunches baby bok choy, quartered lengthwise then cut crosswise into ½-inch (12-mm) thick slices

1 tablespoon tamari

2 teaspoons honey

Steamed rice, for serving

Sliced green onions, including white and green parts, for garnish

Black sesame seeds, for garnish

Put the chicken in a large glass bowl, add the marinade, and toss to coat. Cover and refrigerate for at least 1 hour or overnight.

To cook the chicken, heat the sesame oil in a large sauté pan over medium-high heat. Remove the chicken from the marinade, reserving the marinade, and pat the chicken dry. Add the chicken to the pan skin side down and brown, 3 to 5 minutes. (Because of the sugar in the marinade, the skin will brown very quickly, so watch it carefully.)

Flip the chicken over and add stock to reach halfway up the sides of the chicken, about 1½ cups (360 ml). Reduce the heat to low and simmer with the lid askew for 25 minutes.

Add the bok choy and cook for another 5 minutes, or until the chicken can be easily pierced with a fork and the juices run clear.

Using a slotted spoon, remove the chicken and bok choy from the pan. Add 2 tablespoons of the reserved marinade to the braising liquid, then increase the heat to medium-high. Cook, stirring frequently, until the sauce is reduced by half and has thickened enough to coat the back of a spoon. Taste, adding a little tamari or a squeeze of honey if needed. Return the chicken and bok choy to the pan and turn to coat them with the sauce.

To serve, spoon a mound of rice onto each plate and top with a piece of chicken and some bok choy. Top with a spoonful of the pan juices and a sprinkling of green onions and sesame seeds. Serve right away.

To store: Let cool completely. Refrigerate in an airtight container for up to 3 days.

Mozzarella Chicken Parm

This has become my favorite comfort food recipe. And it's really easy to make! If you don't have time to make the crispy crust on the chicken before baking it, simply cook the chicken on both sides in a little olive oil with salt and pepper before adding to the baking dish.

GF

Prep: 15 minutes

Cook: 25 to 35 minutes

Makes 4 to 6 servings

2 pounds (910 g) boneless, skinless chicken breasts

2 large eggs, beaten

1 cup (125 g) all-purpose flour or gluten-free flour blend, such as Bob's Red Mill 1-to-1 Baking Flour

½ cup (50 g) grated Parmesan

Kosher salt and freshly ground black pepper

5 tablespoons (75 ml) olive oil

One 24-ounce (680-g) jar marinara sauce or tomato-basil sauce

8 ounces (225 g) fresh mozzarella, cut into ⅓-inch- (8-mm-) thick slices

1 cup (145 g) cherry tomatoes

¼ cup (10 g) fresh basil leaves

Preheat the oven to 375°F.

On a cutting board and using a large, sharp knife, cut each chicken breast in half horizontally. Pound each piece of chicken to an even ½-inch (12-mm) thickness with a meat pounder.

Add the eggs to a shallow bowl. In another shallow bowl, combine the flour with ¼ cup (25 g) of the Parmesan; season with salt and pepper. Season the chicken on both sides with salt and pepper.

Using tongs, dip each piece of chicken into the eggs, letting any excess egg drop back into the bowl. Coat with the flour mixture on both sides, shaking off any excess flour. Transfer to a plate and repeat with all the chicken.

In a large nonstick skillet, heat 2 tablespoons of the olive oil over medium-high heat until it's shimmering. Working in two batches and using tongs, cook the chicken, leaving space between each piece, until golden brown and crisp on the bottom, 3 to 4 minutes. Turn the chicken and continue to cook until browned on the other side, 2 to 3 minutes longer. Transfer the chicken to a paper towel–lined plate. Wipe out the pan, add 2 tablespoons of the oil, and repeat to cook the remaining chicken.

In a 9 by 13-inch (23 by 33-cm) baking dish, spread ½ cup (120 ml) of the marinara sauce into an even layer with a rubber spatula. Arrange the chicken pieces on the sauce in a single layer, then pour the remaining sauce around and over the chicken. Top each piece of chicken with some of the fresh mozzarella, then sprinkle with the remaining ¼ cup (25 g) of Parmesan cheese. Sprinkle the cherry tomatoes around the dish, then drizzle the remaining 1 tablespoon of olive oil over it all.

Bake until the cheese has melted and is starting to bubble and the tomatoes have softened a bit, 15 to 20 minutes. Sprinkle with the fresh basil leaves and serve.

Tex-Mex Skillet Casserole

Tori Ritchie is a phenomenal food writer and cookbook author, culinary instructor, and television/video superstar. After I took Tori's food writing class twenty years ago, she became my mentor, encouraging me to write cookbooks. Of all of the recipes I've learned from Tori, this skillet casserole is still my favorite. Tex-Mex at its best, this casserole is the kind of food we all crave, even if we don't want to admit it! Loaded with seasoned ground beef, rice, beans, and topped with cheese, this dish tastes best when eaten around the coffee table with a bag of Fritos while you watch sports on TV. Or roll it up in a tortilla for the tastiest burrito of your life. If you must sit down at the dinner table like civilized adults, serve it up family style out of the pan. Tex-Mex Skillet Casserole, you're basic, and I love you.

GF

Prep: 15 minutes

Cook: 40 minutes

Makes 6 to 8 servings

2 tablespoons olive or avocado oil

1 yellow onion, diced

Kosher salt

3 cloves garlic, minced

1½ pounds (680 g) ground beef

2 tablespoons chili powder

1 cup (185 g) long-grain white rice

One 14-ounce (400-g) can diced tomatoes with juices

One 14-ounce (400-g) can black or pinto beans, drained and rinsed

1 cup (4 ounces/115 g) shredded Cheddar or Monterey Jack cheese

Corn chips and sour cream, for serving (optional)

In a large, ovenproof skillet with a lid, heat the oil over medium-high heat. Add the onion and a generous pinch of salt. Cook, stirring frequently, until the onion is soft, 5 to 8 minutes. Add the garlic and cook until fragrant, about 1 minute. Add the meat and 1 teaspoon of salt and cook, stirring, until the meat is browned and crumbled, 5 to 8 minutes; if desired, drain the fat from the pan. Stir in the chili powder and another generous pinch of salt.

Stir in the rice, tomatoes, beans, and 1½ cups (360 ml) of the water. Bring the mixture to a boil, then reduce the heat to low, cover, and simmer until the rice is cooked through, about 20 minutes. Sprinkle the cheese over the top. If desired, place the pan under a broiler until it has melted, about 1 minute. Serve with corn chips and dollops of sour cream, if desired.

To store: Let cool completely. Refrigerate in an airtight container for up to 3 days.

Raid-the-Fridge Nachos

After twenty years of friendship, my dearest friend, Sunny, and I wound up living on the same block. (It was kismet!) Our families formed a boisterous pod during COVID, so now we're pretty much one big pack. And since her kids eat over here so much, they've been granted professional taste-tester status like my own boys. Sunny's favorite food is nachos, so when we both need a break, I bust out the chips and cheese and get creative from there. We both love Citrusy Pulled Pork (page 183) with them, as well as Pickled Onions (page 46) and Charlie's Guacamole (page 97). The options are endless, but the most important thing about building a good nacho is landing the cheese-to-chip ratio that makes you happy. Sunny and I agree it's about 1:1, meaning every single chip needs solid cheese coverage. But don't take our word for it—make your own!

GF | V | Q!

Prep: 10 minutes

Cook: 5 minutes

Makes 2 to 4 servings

About ½ bag (7 ounces/200 g) thick-cut corn tortilla chips

2 cups (230 g) shredded Cheddar or a mixture of Cheddar and Monterey Jack

One 15-ounce (430-g) can black beans, drained and rinsed

One 4-ounce (115-g) can diced fire-roasted green chiles, drained

———

TOPPINGS (OPTIONAL)

Citrusy Pulled Pork (page 183), warmed

½ cup (120 ml) of your favorite salsa or pico de gallo

¼ cup (60 ml) sour cream

¼ cup (25 g) Pickled Onions (page 46) and/or pickled jalapeños

Charlie's Guacamole (page 97)

In the broiler, position a rack about 6 inches (15 cm) from the heat source and preheat the broiler. Line a baking sheet with aluminum foil or parchment paper.

Arrange the chips in an even layer on the baking sheet, top side up. Sprinkle the chips with all of the cheese or less if you desire. Top evenly with the beans and chiles. Broil until the cheese has melted and the edges of the chips are golden brown, 1 to 3 minutes.

Immediately top the nachos with any of the toppings you like. Serve hot, directly from the baking sheet.

Sheet-Pan Sausage and Polenta with Peppers and Tomatoes

I love Katie Lee Biegel's Cheat Sheet Sausage, Peppers, and Polenta recipe from her book *It's Not Complicated*. It's a sheet-pan dinner that leaves little mess and comes together in a snap! I've adapted Katie's recipe to include roasted cherry tomatoes and a generous dose of fresh basil. Keep this recipe in your back pocket for any night you're in a hurry without a lot of time to cook. To make a vegetarian version of this dish, swap out the sausages for 1 pound of sliced trumpet or portobello mushrooms.

GF | *DF

Prep: 5 minutes

Cook: 30 minutes

Makes 4 servings

4 Italian sausages or other uncooked sausages of your choice (about 1 pound/455 g)

½ red onion, cut into 1-inch (2.5-cm) pieces

2 red and/or yellow bell peppers, seeded and cut into ¼-inch (6-mm) strips

4 tablespoons (60 ml) extra-virgin olive oil

Kosher salt

1 package (16 ounces/455 g) cooked polenta, cut into ½-inch (12-mm) rounds

1 cup (145 g) cherry tomatoes

Freshly cracked black pepper

¼ cup (25 g) grated Parmesan cheese (optional)

¼ cup (10 g) fresh basil leaves, thinly sliced

Position two racks evenly in the oven and preheat to 400°F (205°C).

Put the sausages, onion, and peppers on a baking sheet. Drizzle with 2 tablespoons of the oil and sprinkle with 1 teaspoon salt, tossing lightly with tongs to coat. Roast for 15 minutes.

On a separate baking sheet, arrange the sliced polenta and cherry tomatoes. Drizzle with the remaining 2 tablespoons olive oil and sprinkle with salt and pepper.

Bake until the onions and peppers have softened and the polenta is starting to crisp, about 15 minutes. Sprinkle the polenta with the cheese (if using) and return to the oven. Bake until everything is brown and lightly charred, about 2 minutes longer.

Serve directly from the baking sheets or arrange the polenta and tomatoes in a large, wide serving dish or platter and top with the sausage-pepper mixture. Sprinkle with the fresh basil and serve immediately.

To store: Let cool completely. Refrigerate in an airtight container for up to 3 days.

Apple Cider–Brined Pork Chops

I love pork chops. Their mild, sweet flavor pairs well with so many other foods. Brining them to add flavor and tenderness is my favorite trick. I typically serve chops with a salad with apples or pears in it, but the Warm Brussels Sprouts, Cabbage, and Apple "Slaw" (page 144) is my new favorite pairing. The slaw is delicious on its own, but save some to reheat with the pork chops and you'll be in heaven.

GF | DF

Prep: 15 minutes, plus 4 to 16 hours brining

Cook: 20 to 30 minutes

Makes 4 servings

BRINE

¼ cup (45 g) kosher salt

½ cup (120 ml) apple cider

3 pods star anise

1 cinnamon stick

4 whole cloves

8 black peppercorns, smashed

1-inch (2.5-cm) piece fresh ginger, smashed

———————

Four 6- to 8-ounce (170- to 225-g) bone-in single-cut pork chops

2 tablespoons olive oil

To make the brine, in a large saucepan, combine the salt with 2 cups (480 ml) warm water. Heat over medium-high heat until the salt dissolves. Remove from the heat and add the apple cider, star anise, cinnamon stick, cloves, peppercorns, and ginger. Stir to combine and let steep for a few minutes. Add enough ice (about 4 cups/600 g) to cool the brine to room temperature. Once the brine is cool, add enough additional cold water to equal 2 quarts (2 l) of liquid. Use the brine now or cover and refrigerate for up to 5 days.

Put the pork chops in a lidded glass or ceramic dish or large resealable storage bag. Pour the brine over the chops and ensure they are submerged. Refrigerate for at least 4 hours or up to overnight, turning the chops once or twice.

One hour before grilling, remove the pork chops from the brine. Rinse them under cool water and pat dry. Discard the brine. Let the pork chops sit at room temperature for 1 hour.

Prepare a grill for direct cooking over medium-high heat (about 400°F/205°C). Brush the grill grate clean.

Brush the pork chops with the olive oil. Place the pork chops over direct heat, cover the grill, and cook for 7 minutes without opening the grill. Flip the pork chops and cook until the internal temperature reaches 150°F (66°C) on an instant-read thermometer, 5 to 12 minutes. Transfer to a cutting board and let rest for 10 minutes before serving.

To store: Let cool completely. Refrigerate in an airtight container for up to 3 days.

Five-Star Five-Spice Ribs

When I started teaching cooking classes out of my own kitchen for local moms over fifteen years ago, one of the first requests I had was to teach them how to make ribs. If I had a dollar for every time I heard, "My husband doesn't know how to make them, so I want to learn," I'd have a second home in Italy by now. Guess what? They're easy to make, and you don't have to smoke them! Once you learn the technique, you'll be making these bad boys any time you catch a craving. Pro tip? Ask your butcher to trim the ribs of the silver skin on the back of each rack if they haven't already. You can certainly keep it on, but removing it allows you to enjoy more of the meat on each rib. I prefer St. Louis–style ribs over babyback ribs because they've got more meat and are a little fattier, which in my mind are the two things that constitute a tasty rib!

GF | DF

Prep: 20 minutes

Cook: 2 to 3 hours

Makes 6 to 8 servings

2 racks (about 7 pounds/ 3.2 kg) St. Louis–style pork ribs, trimmed of silver skin

Kosher salt and freshly ground black pepper

1 cup (240 ml) apple cider or water

½ cup (120 ml) Five-Spice BBQ Sauce (page 52) or your favorite store-bought barbecue sauce, plus more if desired

TIP: To reduce the grill temp on a charcoal grill, you can leave the damper halfway open for medium heat between 350°–450°F (175°–230°C) and a quarter open for low heat between 250°–350°F (120°–175°C.

Prepare a grill for indirect cooking over medium-low heat (300°F/150°C) or preheat the oven to 300°F (150°C). Season each rack of ribs on both sides with 1 tablespoon salt and a few grindings of pepper.

Tear off three long sheets of heavy-duty aluminum foil. The foil should be at least a foot longer than the ribs. Arrange the foil sheets on a heavy, rimmed baking sheet, overlapping them by a few inches, so they cover the pan and are wide enough to completely enclose the ribs. Place both rib racks on the foil, one on top of the other, pulling up the sides of the foil to keep the liquid inside. Pour the apple cider around the ribs. Place a fourth piece of foil on top and crimp all of the edges together to prevent leaking.

Place the pan on the grill (with the grill closed) or in the oven and cook until the ribs are fork-tender but not falling off the bone, 2 to 3 hours.

Reduce the grill or oven temperature to 225°F (110°C). Carefully remove the ribs from the foil. Save the juices, if desired, to strain and serve mixed with extra BBQ sauce.

Brush the ribs on both sides with the BBQ sauce. Place the ribs over direct heat on the grill grate or return to the baking sheet and place in the oven. Cook until the sauce thickens on the ribs, about 10 minutes. Transfer to a cutting board and let cool slightly. Cut into individual ribs and serve with BBQ sauce on the side.

Citrusy Pulled Pork

Years ago, I learned how to make cochinita pibil, a Yucatán pork dish cooked in banana leaves. The banana leaves help lock in the juices and braise the pork—much like a Dutch oven functions in this recipe. The hand-ground spices help create a flavorful pulled pork to serve over rice and beans or as a filling for tacos, enchiladas, and more. Over the past two decades, I've continued to simplify the ingredients and method to create a recipe that takes only minutes to prep. This dish cooks slowly but surely in your oven, but you can also use a slow cooker. Because this is so easy to cook and makes such a large portion of pulled pork, it's my favorite to serve when I entertain. Paired with rice and black beans, you have the perfect meal!

GF | DF | MA

Prep: 15 minutes

Cook: 2½ to 3½ hours

Makes 8 to 10 servings

6 pounds (2.7 kg) boneless pork shoulder (pork butt)

Kosher salt

1 cup (240 ml) fresh orange juice

½ cup (120 ml) fresh lime juice

Achiote Marinade (page 60)

3 cloves garlic, crushed

3 tablespoons olive oil

1 cup (240 ml) chicken stock (page 43), if needed

———————

ACCOMPANIMENTS (OPTIONAL)

Corn tortillas, warmed

Pickled Onions (page 46)

Charlie's Guacamole (page 97)

Your favorite salsa or pico de gallo

1 cup (240 ml) Mexican crema

Lime wedges

Cut the pork shoulder into 4-inch- (10-cm-) thick slices. Trim off any excess fat on the outside of the pork. (The meat itself should be well marbled.) Season the meat all over with 1 tablespoon salt. Put the pork in a Dutch oven or other heavy pot with a tight-fitting lid.

In a medium bowl, combine the orange juice, lime juice, marinade, and the garlic. Pour the mixture over the pork along with the olive oil, turning the pork with tongs to make sure it is covered in the marinade. Add the stock if needed to ensure the marinade is halfway up the sides of the pot. Let the pork marinate for 1 hour at room temperature or up to overnight in the refrigerator, turning once. (If refrigerating, remove from the refrigerator 1 hour before cooking.)

Preheat the oven to 350°F (175°C). Cover the pot and bake until fork-tender and starting to fall apart, 2½ to 3½ hours.

Transfer the pork to a cutting board or platter, reserving the cooking liquid. When cool enough to handle, shred the pork, discarding any large pieces of fat as you go. Transfer the shredded pork to a bowl. Skim any fat from the cooking liquid, strain the liquid through a fine-mesh sieve set over a bowl, and then use the cooking liquid to moisten the pork. Taste, adding more salt to the pork if needed.

Serve hot, with some or all of the accompaniments alongside.

Sunday Meatballs and "Sauce"

A16 is my favorite Italian restaurant in San Francisco. Their award-winning Italian wine selection, wood-fired pizzas, pastas, and roasted meats and veggies have kept A16 at the forefront of the local dining scene for over fifteen years. Early in its inception, the restaurant started hosting Monday Night Meatball nights, and my friends and family became hooked. While testing the recipes for their cookbook, I learned to make these pillowy, perfectly seasoned meatballs. I've simplified the ingredient list and method so you can enjoy them no matter where you live. I must warn you, this is going to be a messy endeavor, but they are so dang good it is worth it every time!

*GF | MA

Prep: 30 minutes

Cook: 1½ to 2½ hours

Makes 4 to 6 servings

1 cup (245 g) fresh ricotta

1 pound (455 g) ground pork

1 pound (455 g) ground beef (80 percent lean)

4 cups (9 g) fresh bread crumbs (see page 65), regular or gluten-free

½ bunch fresh flat-leaf parsley, stemmed and coarsely chopped (about 2 cups/100 g)

Kosher salt

1 tablespoon dried oregano

2 teaspoons fennel seeds

1 teaspoon red pepper flakes

4 large eggs, lightly beaten

½ cup (120 ml) whole milk

Extra-virgin olive oil

One 15-ounce (430-g) can diced San Marzano tomatoes with juice

One 15-ounce (430-g) can crushed tomatoes

½ bunch fresh basil leaves (about ½ cup/15 g loosely packed)

½ cup (50 g) freshly grated Parmesan

Preheat the oven to 400°F (205°C). Line two baking sheets with parchment paper. Put the ricotta in a fine-mesh sieve set over a bowl to drain for 15 minutes.

In a large bowl, combine the pork, beef, bread crumbs, parsley, 2 tablespoons salt, the oregano, fennel seeds, and pepper flakes. Mix gently with your hands just until all of the ingredients are evenly distributed. Set aside.

In a separate bowl, whisk together the drained ricotta, eggs, and milk just enough to break up any large curds of ricotta. Add the ricotta mixture to the ground meat mixture and mix gently with your hands until incorporated. The mixture should feel wet and tacky. (It will be looser and tackier than you'd expect a meatball to be.)

To test for proper seasoning, heat a small skillet over medium heat. Add a drizzle of olive oil to the pan. Pinch off a small piece of the mixture, flatten it into a disc, and cook it on both sides until cooked through. Taste the meat, then add more salt to the mixture if desired and mix lightly with your hands. (Make a note of how much salt you used in your recipe so you can skip this step the next time.)

Form the meat mixture into 1½-inch (4-cm) balls, each weighing about 2 ounces (55 g). Place the meatballs a few inches apart on the prepared pans. You will have about 3 dozen meatballs.

Place the baking sheets in the oven and bake the meatballs, rotating the sheets once from front to back, until the meatballs are browned and barely cooked through, 15 to 25 minutes. (Cut one open to check). Remove from the oven and let cool for a minute, then transfer the meatballs to a roasting pan. Reduce the oven temperature to 300°F (150°C).

In a medium bowl, combine the diced and crushed tomatoes, 1 tablespoon salt, and 2 tablespoons olive oil. Stir to combine.

Pour the tomato sauce over the meatballs, cover tightly with aluminum foil, and bake until the meatballs are fluffy and tender and have absorbed some of the tomato sauce, 1 to 1½ hours.

Uncover the pans and distribute the basil leaves throughout the sauce. Sprinkle the Parmesan over the top, drizzle with olive oil to finish, and serve immediately.

To store: Let cool completely. Refrigerate in an airtight container for up to 3 days.

> NOTE: The meatballs freeze really well if you bake them without the sauce. Freeze the baked meatballs on a small baking sheet, then transfer to an airtight container and freeze for up to 1 month. To use, defrost at room temperature for 1 hour, then add the tomato sauce and bake according to the recipe.

Grilled Skirt Steak with Chimichurri

This is my most requested recipe of all time. The secret to this recipe is its simplicity. When you use great ingredients, they don't need to be dressed up. Letting the steak come to room temperature before cooking ensures it will cook evenly throughout. The fresh herbs, garlic, and citrus of the chimichurri cut through the richness of the steak, making it the perfect sauce pairing. Because this dish is so easy to make, I keep my sides simple, too. Herb-Smothered Potatoes (page 135) are a delicious option, or see my tip below for roasting sweet potatoes while you make the steak and chimichurri. If you can't find skirt steak, flap steak or hanger steak are great alternatives.

GF | DF | Q!

Prep: 5 minutes

Cook: 10 minutes

Makes 4 servings

2 pounds (910 g) skirt steak, trimmed and cut into 6- to 8-inch (15- to 20-cm) steaks

Olive oil

Kosher salt and freshly ground black pepper

Chimichurri (page 49)

> **TIP:** To roast sweet potatoes (I like the bright orange garnets), while the steaks are coming to room temp, preheat the oven to 400°F (205°C). Prick each potato a few times with a fork. Brush the skins with a little olive oil. Place on a parchment paper–lined baking sheet and bake until the potatoes are knife-tender, 40 to 50 minutes. Let cool for 10 minutes, then cut open and serve with extra chimichurri sauce.

One hour before serving, remove the steaks from the refrigerator to let them come to room temperature.

Prepare a grill for direct cooking over medium-high heat (about 400°F/205°C). Brush the grill grate clean and lightly oil the grate.

Rub each steak with oil, then season generously all over with salt and pepper. Grill the steaks over direct heat, 4 to 5 minutes per side for medium-rare, or until the internal temperature of the steak reaches 130°F (54°C) on an instant-read thermometer. Transfer to a cutting board, tent with aluminum foil, and let rest for 10 minutes.

Slice the steaks against the grain, then arrange on a platter. Pour the chimichurri over the steaks and serve additional sauce on the side.

Herb-Explosion Burgers

Nine times out of ten, I add just salt and pepper to ground beef when I'm making burgers. Why? Because when you buy good ingredients, they don't need a lot of seasoning! However, when I want to add a little extra flavor without overpowering the meat, I use this recipe. The most important thing to remember when making a burger? Your meat must be well seasoned. If you're not sure if you're using the right amount of salt, cook off a tiny piece in a pan to see if you like the seasoning. If you think it needs more, you can then add more to the raw meat mixture before shaping it into patties.

°GF | °DF | Q!

Prep: 5 to 10 minutes

Cook: 10 minutes

Makes 4 servings

1 pound (455 g) ground beef (preferably 80/20 percent fat)

1 shallot, minced

2 tablespoons finely chopped fresh herbs, such as flat-leaf parsley, basil, mint, and/or tarragon

1 tablespoon capers, drained and finely chopped

Kosher salt and freshly ground black pepper

4 slices cheddar or havarti cheese (optional)

4 hamburger buns, regular or gluten-free, split

Your favorite condiments

4 thick slices ripe tomato

4 lettuce leaves

Prepare a grill for direct cooking over medium-high heat. Brush the grill grate clean. Line a small baking sheet with parchment paper.

In a large bowl, combine the ground beef, shallot, herbs, capers, 1 teaspoon salt, and ½ teaspoon pepper. Gently mix with your hands. Do not overwork the meat. Divide the mixture into four equal balls. Press into ½-inch- (12-mm-) thick patties and transfer to the prepared baking sheet. (If not cooking immediately, cover and refrigerate for up to 8 hours.)

Using a metal spatula, transfer the patties to the grill and set over direct heat until well browned, 2 to 3 minutes per side for medium-rare. Top with cheese during the last minute of cooking, if desired. Transfer the patties to a plate to rest for 3 minutes. Toast the buns on the grill, cut sides down, while the burgers rest.

Build each burger with your favorite condiments, layering the patty, tomato, and lettuce on the bottom half of the bun. Add the burger top and serve immediately.

Sweets are for Sundays

CHAPTER EIGHT

Is sugar bad for us? Yes! Do I want to get rid of desserts? Heck, no! Sugar is everywhere, in everything, and basically does nothing good for us. But I live in the real world, and I don't want to be deprived of treats. So, my solution is to cook something wonderful once a week and just dig in and enjoy it. We all deserve a little sunshine in our lives, and if yours comes in the form of a Barely Better-for-You Lemon Bar (page 204), or a few of Stevey's Caramel Apple–Oat Chews (page 194), then good on you! Lick your fingers and enjoy every bite.

Vanilla Cheesecake with Strawberries

Cheesecake might be my favorite dessert, next to lemon bars. (Can I pick two?) I grew up eating cheesecake with a thin layer of sweetened sour cream spread over the top. I still love it, but you can delete it in this recipe, if you like. Try using fresh blueberries in place of the strawberries or add 1 teaspoon Autumn Spice Blend (page 64) to the batter and drizzle with caramel instead of the fruit topping. Or make it gluten-free with gluten-free graham cracker crumbs. Any way you enjoy it, you can master this basic recipe to make it your own!

°GF | V | MA

Prep: 15 minutes, plus 4 hours to overnight to cool and set

Cook: 50 to 60 minutes

Makes 12 servings

CRUST

1½ cups (180 g) finely ground graham cracker crumbs (about 5 double graham crackers)

¼ cup (55 g) light brown sugar, packed

3 tablespoons unsalted butter, melted

FILLING

2 pounds (910 g) cream cheese, at room temperature

1 cup (200 g) granulated sugar

1 teaspoon pure vanilla extract, or beans from 1 vanilla bean

4 large eggs

SOUR CREAM TOPPING (optional)

1 pint (16 ounces/480 ml) sour cream

3 tablespoons granulated sugar

1 teaspoon pure vanilla extract

STRAWBERRY TOPPING

3 cups (about 1 pound/455 g) fresh strawberries, sliced

1 teaspoon finely grated lemon zest

1 to 3 teaspoons granulated sugar

Preheat the oven to 325°F (165°C).

For the crust: In a medium bowl, combine the graham cracker crumbs, brown sugar, and butter in a bowl. Stir to combine. Press the crumb mixture evenly into the bottom of a 9-inch (23-cm) springform pan.

For the filling: In the bowl of a stand mixer fitted with the paddle attachment, combine the cream cheese, granulated sugar, and vanilla. Beat on medium speed until smooth, stopping a few times to scrape down the sides with a rubber spatula. With the mixer on low, add the eggs one at a time, beating until fully incorporated and stopping again to scrape down the sides if necessary.

Pour the filling into the springform pan, using a rubber spatula to smooth the top. Bake until the center is barely set, 50 to 60 minutes. Let cool completely on a wire rack.

To make the optional sour cream topping: In a medium bowl, combine the sour cream, sugar, and vanilla. Stir well to blend. Spread the mixture over the top of the cheesecake, then refrigerate for at least 3 hours or up to overnight to set the topping.

Just before serving, make the strawberry topping: In a bowl, combine the strawberries, lemon zest, and 1 teaspoon sugar. Taste, adding a little more sugar if desired. Top the cheesecake with the strawberries and serve at once.

To store: Refrigerate the cheesecake and strawberries, covered or in an airtight container, for up to 2 days.

Stevey's Caramel Apple–Oat Chews

This may be the best non-chocolate cookie anywhere. My dearest, oldest friend Denise met her husband Steve when we moved to San Francisco together after college graduation. "Stevey" became a frequent dinner guest at our apartment and my most eager taste-tester. He fell in love with these cookies I would make for him and talked endlessly about how much he adored the combination of the apples with the caramel in cookie form. Twenty-five years later, Steve is still so enthused about my cooking that I decided to bring this cookie back just for him. I have to admit, there really is something magical about the combination of oats, fresh apple, and sticky caramel that is unbeatable. It's like eating a more exciting—and less messy—version of a caramel apple. Stevey: here's to many more years of enjoying these cookies together!

°GF | V | Q!

Prep: 15 minutes

Cook: 10 to 13 minutes

Makes 30 cookies

1½ cups (135 g) gluten-free old-fashioned rolled oats, such as Bob's Red Mill brand

1½ cups (190 g) all-purpose flour or gluten-free flour blend, such as Bob's Red Mill 1-to-1 Baking Flour

¾ teaspoon baking soda

½ teaspoon ground cinnamon

Pinch of kosher salt

1 cup (2 sticks/225 g) unsalted butter, at room temperature

1 cup (220 g) light brown sugar, firmly packed

2 large eggs, lightly beaten

1 tablespoon whole milk

1 teaspoon pure vanilla extract

1½ cups (240 g) diced peeled apple (about 2 apples), such as Granny Smith or Honeycrisp

½ cup (120 ml) jarred caramel sauce

Position two racks evenly in the oven and preheat to 325°F (165°C). Line two baking sheets with parchment paper.

In a medium bowl, combine the oats, flour, baking soda, cinnamon, and salt. Stir with a whisk to blend.

In a stand mixer, beat together the butter and sugar on medium speed until light and fluffy, 3 to 5 minutes. Scrape down the sides with a rubber spatula, then add the eggs, milk, and vanilla and mix until incorporated. Add half of the dry ingredients and mix on low speed just until incorporated. Add the remaining dry ingredients and mix just until incorporated. Fold in the apples.

Using a small ice cream scoop or a tablespoon, scoop up about 2 tablespoons of the dough and drop them on the prepared pans, spacing them a few inches apart. Bake until the bottoms are just beginning to turn golden brown, 10 to 13 minutes.

Let the cookies cool on the pan on a wire rack for 15 minutes, then transfer to the rack to cool completely.

Warm the caramel sauce according to the manufacturer's instructions. Using the tines of a fork or a small spoon, drizzle the caramel over the cookies. Let cool for a few minutes to set, then serve.

To store: Arrange in a single layer in an airtight container, and store at room temperature for up to 3 days.

Chocolate-Toffee Crinkle Cookies

Leave it to Caitlin, my amazing culinary assistant, to take a favorite recipe of mine and make it better. I started making chocolate crinkle cookies often when I found out that I was gluten-intolerant, since cocoa powder helps to improve the texture of cookies made with gluten-free flour. With regular or gluten-free flour, toffee chunks make these cookies special.

°GF | V | MA

Prep: 15 minutes

Cook: 15 minutes

Makes 18 cookies

1 cup (125 g) all-purpose flour or gluten-free flour blend, such as Bob's Red Mill 1-to-1 Baking Flour

¾ cup (70 g) unsweetened Dutch-process cocoa powder

½ teaspoon baking powder

¼ teaspoon salt

½ cup (1 stick/115 g) unsalted butter, at room temperature

½ cup (100 g) granulated sugar

¼ cup (55 g) light brown sugar, firmly packed

2 large eggs

1 teaspoon pure vanilla extract

¾ cup (280 g) crushed toffee bits

½ cup (50 g) confectioners' sugar, sifted

Position two racks evenly in the oven and preheat to 350°F (175°C). Line two baking sheets with parchment paper.

In a medium bowl, combine the flour, cocoa powder, baking powder, and salt. Stir with a whisk to blend. Set aside.

In a stand mixer, beat together the butter and sugars on medium speed until light and fluffy, 3 to 5 minutes. Scrape down the sides with a rubber spatula. Add the eggs one at a time, then add the vanilla and mix until incorporated. Turn the speed down to low and add half of the dry ingredients until just incorporated before adding the other half. Fold in the toffee bits. Refrigerate the dough for 10 to 15 minutes.

Put the confectioners' sugar into in a shallow bowl. Using a small ice cream scoop or a tablespoon, scoop up about 2 tablespoonfuls of the dough and roll it into a ball, then roll the ball in the confectioners' sugar, coating it completely. Arrange the balls on prepared pans about 2 inches (5 cm) apart. Repeat with the remaining dough.

Bake until puffed, rotating the pans between the racks halfway through baking, 10 to 12 minutes.

Let the cookies cool on the pans for about 15 minutes, then transfer to a wire rack to continue cooling.

To store: Store in an airtight container at room temperature for up to 3 days.

Citrus–Olive Oil Cake

Recently, I created an entire olive oil menu for an olive oil commercial, and when asked to develop a dessert, I immediately knew I wanted to make an olive oil cake. A little added cornmeal adds a bit of crunch to this one, and the fresh orange juice and fragrant orange zest brings it all together. The olive oil gives it a silky texture (and is better for you than butter!), and the not-too-sweet hint of orange keeps you wanting more. This showstopper of a cake was so well-loved that I ended up making it three times in one week!

V | MA

Prep: 10 minutes
Cook: 1 hour, plus time to cool
Makes 8 to 12

1½ cups (190 g) all-purpose flour

1½ cups (300 g) sugar

½ cup (90 g) fine cornmeal

1½ teaspoons kosher salt

½ teaspoon baking soda

1⅓ cups (315 ml) extra-virgin olive oil

3 large eggs, separated

1¼ cups (300 ml) whole milk

1½ tablespoons grated orange zest (about 1 orange)

½ cup (120 ml) fresh orange juice

1 teaspoon pure vanilla extract

2 navel or blood oranges

1 cup (240 ml) crème fraîche or sour cream

2 teaspoons light brown sugar

Preheat the oven to 350°F (175°C). Line a 9-inch (23-cm) round cake pan with parchment paper, then spray the pan with nonstick cooking spray.

In a large bowl, combine the flour, sugar, cornmeal, salt, and baking soda. Whisk to combine.

In a medium bowl, whisk the olive oil with the egg yolks until they are combined and emulsified, 30 to 60 seconds. Add the egg whites, milk, orange zest, orange juice, and vanilla and whisk until thoroughly combined.

Pour the liquid ingredients into the dry ingredients, whisking just until the lumps are gone. Pour the batter into the prepared cake pan and bake until golden brown on top and a toothpick comes out clean when inserted into the center of the cake, about 1 hour. (If the cake becomes too brown before it is done cooking, lightly tent it with aluminum foil to prevent further browning.)

Let the cake cool in the pan for 5 minutes before inverting it onto a wire rack and peeling off the parchment paper.

While the cake bakes, prepare the orange slices. Using a sharp knife, cut a slice off both ends of each orange down to the flesh. Stand the orange upright on a cutting board and cut downward, following the contour of the orange, to remove the peel and white pith. Cut between the membranes to segment the orange or slice the fruit crosswise, picking out any seeds. Transfer to a bowl.

When ready to serve, in a small bowl, stir together the crème fraîche and brown sugar. Slide the cake onto a cake plate. Cut into wedges and serve with a dollop of the sweetened crème fraîche and a spoonful of the oranges and their juice.

S'mores Bars

These bars have never lasted for more than a few hours in my house, and for good reason: They bring the popular combo of chocolate, graham crackers, and marshmallows to the table in the form of an easy-to-eat cookie. Once you master the crust—one of the easiest bases for a sweet treat you can make—you can add different ingredients to the chocolate mixture by substituting macadamia nuts for the walnuts, or even stirring in ½ cup (85 g) of butterscotch chips along with the marshmallows. You can easily make these gluten-free by using gluten-free graham cracker crumbs.

*GF | V | MA

Prep: 20 minutes

Cook: 30 minutes, plus 2 hours to chill

Makes 16 bars

CRUST

1½ cups (180 g) finely ground graham cracker crumbs (about 5 double graham crackers)

¾ cup (95 g) all-purpose flour or gluten-free flour blend, such as Bob's Red Mill 1-to-1 Baking Flour

½ cup (110 g) brown sugar, firmly packed

Pinch of kosher salt

½ cup (1 stick/115 g) cold unsalted butter, cut into ½-inch (12-mm) cubes

1 large egg, lightly beaten

TOPPING

⅔ cup (165 ml) heavy cream

12 ounces (340 g) dark chocolate chips or chunks, such as Guittard or Callebaut

2 cups (100 g) miniature marshmallows

⅓ cup (40 g) chopped walnuts, toasted (see page 65), optional

Flaky salt, for garnish (optional)

Preheat the oven to 350°F (175°C). Line a 9-inch (23-cm) square baking pan with parchment paper.

For the crust: To the bowl of a food processor fitted with the metal blade, add the graham cracker crumbs, flour, brown sugar, and salt. Pulse a few times to incorporate. Add the butter pieces and process until the mixture resembles coarse meal, then add the egg and pulse a few times until the mixture sticks together.

Transfer the mixture to the prepared pan and, using lightly buttered fingers, press evenly into the bottom to form a crust. Alternatively, use the flat bottom of a measuring cup or glass to press the mixture into the pan.

Bake until golden brown and just firm to the touch, 18 to 20 minutes. Let cool completely in the pan on a wire rack, about 30 minutes.

For the topping: In a medium saucepan, bring the cream to a simmer over medium-low heat (do not boil). Remove from the heat, add the chocolate, and whisk until melted and smooth. Stir in the marshmallows and the walnuts, if using. Spread the mixture evenly over the crust, then cover and refrigerate until firm, about 2 hours.

Use the parchment to lift the sheet from the pan, then cut the bars into 2-inch (5-cm) squares. Sprinkle with a little flaky salt, if desired.

To store: Remove from the parchment, arrange in a single layer in an airtight container, and refrigerate for up to 3 days.

Poppy Seed Bundt Cake with Lemon-Berry Glaze

This is my riff on a classic poppy seed bundt cake that my mom made for special celebrations when I was growing up. My modern take includes pureed berries in the glaze, almost guaranteeing this will be the most stunning cake you've ever served! In addition, it's absolutely delicious with either gluten-free or standard cake flour. So let them ALL eat cake!

*GF | V | MA

Prep: 15 minutes, plus 1 hour to cool and glaze

Cook: 40 to 50 minutes

Makes 10 to 12 servings

POPPY SEED BUNDT CAKE

¾ cup (180 ml) whole milk

⅓ cup (190 g) poppy seeds

1½ teaspoons pure vanilla extract

2 cups (260 g) cake flour (regular or gluten-free) or gluten-free flour blend, such as Bob's Red Mill 1-to-1 Baking Flour

2½ teaspoons baking powder

¼ teaspoon kosher salt

¾ cup (170 g) unsalted butter, at room temperature

1½ cups (300 g) granulated sugar

4 large egg whites

GLAZE AND TOPPING

2 cups (200 g) confectioners' sugar, sifted

½ cup (120 ml) seedless berry puree (see Note)

¼ cup (60 ml) fresh lemon juice

2 cups (280 g) fresh berries

NOTE: To make seedless berry puree, blend 1 cup (140 g) of defrosted frozen blackberries or raspberries in a blender until smooth, then press them through a fine-mesh sieve.

To make the cake, in a small bowl, combine the milk, poppy seeds, and vanilla. Set aside to soak for 1 hour.

Preheat the oven to 375°F (190°C). Butter and flour a standard-sized Bundt pan, shaking out any excess flour.

In a small bowl, combine the flour, baking powder, and salt. Stir with a whisk to blend.

In the bowl of a stand mixer, beat the butter on medium speed until soft and creamy, then add the granulated sugar. Mix until fluffy, scraping down the sides of the bowl with a rubber spatula as necessary. Reduce the speed to low and gradually add half the milk mixture. Add half of the flour mixture and beat on low speed just until combined. Repeat with the remaining milk mixture and flour mixture, mixing just until combined.

In a large bowl, using clean beaters, beat the egg whites to medium-stiff peaks. Using a rubber spatula, gently fold the egg whites into the cake batter until they're incorporated.

Pour the batter into the pan and gently smooth the top with a rubber spatula. Bake until a toothpick inserted in the center of the cake comes out clean, 40 to 50 minutes. Let cool in the pan on a wire rack for 10 minutes, then invert the cake onto a cake plate or stand and let cool completely, about 45 minutes.

To make the glaze, in a small bowl, stir together the confectioners' sugar, berry puree, and lemon juice until smooth. Using a toothpick, poke 20 to 30 holes in the top of the cake. Gradually pour the glaze over the top of the cake. Garnish with the fresh berries and serve, cut into wedges.

To store: Store the cake, covered or in an airtight container, at room temperature for up to 3 days. Store any leftover berry puree in the refrigerator for up to 3 days.

Pear-Blueberry Crisp (aka "A Crisp for All Seasons")

If you love fruit crisps as much as I do, make it a point to double the topping and freeze half of it so you've got some ready to go whenever you bring home fresh, seasonal fruit! I love this pear and blueberry combo for fall, but you can mix and match any fruits you like, especially in the summer when ripe peaches, nectarines, plums, and berries are at the market.

*GF | *DF | **VG | V

Prep: 20 minutes
Cook: 30 to 40 minutes
Makes 8 servings

TOPPING

1 cup (90 g) gluten-free old-fashioned rolled oats, such as Bob's Red Mill brand

½ cup (65 g) all-purpose flour or gluten-free flour blend, such as Bob's Red Mill 1-to-1 Baking Flour

¼ cup (30 g) almond flour

⅓ cup (75 g) light brown sugar, firmly packed

½ teaspoon ground cinnamon

¼ teaspoon kosher salt

6 tablespoons (85 g) cold unsalted butter or vegan butter, cut into 6 slices

———————

3 ripe pears, peeled, cored and chopped (about 3 cups/540 g)

2 cups (290 g) fresh blueberries

1 tablespoon fresh lemon juice

½ teaspoon pure vanilla extract

Pinch of kosher salt

1 to 2 tablespoons granulated sugar

Whipped cream (facing page) or vanilla bean ice cream, for serving (optional)

Preheat the oven to 350°F (175°C).

For the topping: In a large bowl, combine the oats, flours, brown sugar, cinnamon, and salt; stir to blend. Add the butter and use a pastry blender or fork to cut the butter into pea-size pieces. Refrigerate until ready to use, up to overnight.

In a medium bowl, combine the fruit, lemon juice, vanilla, and salt. Taste and add the sugar only as needed, 1 tablespoon at a time.

Transfer the fruit mixture to a 9-inch (23-cm) square baking pan, then sprinkle evenly with the crisp topping. Bake until brown and bubbly, 30 to 40 minutes. If the top becomes too brown before it is bubbling around the edges, cover with aluminum foil and cook for 5 to 10 minutes longer. Let cool on a wire rack for about 20 minutes.

Using a large spoon, scoop out servings. Top with a dollop of whipped cream or a scoop of ice cream if you like.

To store: Let cool completely. Refrigerate, covered or in an airtight container, for up to 3 days.

Whipped Cream

Homemade whipped cream is quick and easy to make, and the difference in taste from canned whipped cream is unbelievable. You can use an electric mixer or a large whisk and a large bowl. Chilling the bowl and metal whisk attachment in the fridge for 30 minutes will help the cream whip faster.

GF | V | Q!

Prep: 7 to 10 minutes

Makes about 2 cups (240 ml)

1 cup (240 ml) heavy cream

1 to 2 tablespoons confectioners' sugar, pushed through a fine-mesh sieve

1 teaspoon pure vanilla extract (optional)

TIP: What's the difference between a soft peak and a medium peak? When you dip the wire whisk attachment or a whisk into the whipped cream, a soft peak will fall back into the bowl. A medium peak will curl over like soft-serve ice cream but hold onto the whisk. If you overwhip your cream and it starts to look curdled, simply add 1 tablespoon of heavy cream to the mixture and beat on low speed until it begins to come back together.

In a large bowl, using an electric mixer fitted with the whisk attachment, beat the cream, 1 tablespoon sugar, and the vanilla (if using) on medium-high speed until soft peaks form; be careful to not overwhip. Taste, adding more sugar if desired. Continue to beat on medium-high speed until medium peaks form. Use at once or cover and refrigerate for up to 3 hours. Lightly beat the whipped cream before using.

Alternatively, beat the whipped cream by hand. In a medium bowl, combine the cream, 1 tablespoon sugar, and the vanilla (if using). Using a large balloon whisk, beat the mixture until soft peaks form, being careful not to overwhip.

Barely Better-for-You Lemon Bars

I love asking people what they'd choose for their last meal. Mine would be a smorgasbord including chicken tacos from my favorite taqueria, a bone-in rib eye with a pile of fries, a perfect slice of pizza, and for dessert, this lemon bar would definitively be my last sweet treat here on Earth. Half buttery shortbread and half lemon curd, no one is going to call these bars healthy, but they are satisfyingly smooth and buttery, and absolutely worth making. Plus, they have massive amounts of vitamin C! I love using Meyer lemons, which are a little less tart than a typical lemon, but use whatever type of lemon you prefer.

*GF | V | MA

Prep: 20 minutes, plus 1 hour cooling time

Cook: 50 to 60 minutes

Makes 24 bars

SHORTBREAD CRUST

2 cups (250 g) all-purpose flour or gluten-free flour blend, such as Bob's Red Mill 1-to-1 Baking Flour

1 cup (115 g) finely ground almond flour

1 cup (125 g) confectioners' sugar

Pinch of kosher salt

1½ cups (3 sticks/340 g) unsalted butter, at room temperature

LEMON CURD FILLING

2¼ cups (450 g) granulated sugar

3 tablespoons all-purpose flour or gluten-free flour blend, such as Bob's Red Mill 1-to-1 Baking Flour

1 tablespoon grated lemon zest

¼ teaspoon kosher salt

¾ cup (180 ml) fresh lemon juice (about 3 lemons)

6 large eggs

Confectioners' sugar, for dusting

Preheat the oven to 350°F (175°C). Line a 9 by 13-inch (23 by 33-cm) rimmed baking sheet with aluminum foil, leaving a 2-inch (5-cm) overhang on the shorter sides of the pan.

For the crust: In a large mixing bowl or in the bowl of a stand mixer, combine the flour, almond flour, confectioners' sugar, and a pinch of salt. Stir with a whisk to blend. Work the butter into the flour mixture with your hands or on low speed until it resembles coarse meal. The mixture should hold together when pressed together with your fingers but remain easily crumbled.

Using the bottom of a drinking glass, press the dough into the pan to form an even layer. If the dough becomes too warm, place the pan in the freezer for 3 minutes to chill the dough, then resume pressing it into the bottom of the pan.

Bake the crust until lightly golden and dry in appearance throughout, 30 to 35 minutes. Remove from the oven, transfer the pan to a wire rack, and let the crust cool completely, about 1 hour.

While the crust cools, make the filling: Combine the sugar, flour, lemon zest, and salt in a large bowl. Stir with a whisk to blend. Add the lemon juice and whisk until blended. Add the eggs, one at a time, whisking to incorporate each egg fully before adding another. Pour the filling over the crust. Bake until the filling is set and looks slightly dry on top, 20 to 25 minutes. Let cool completely in the pan on a wire rack.

Sift 2 tablespoons confectioners' sugar over the top of the cooled lemon bars. To serve, lift the bars from the pan using the foil "handles" and cut into 24 bars.

ACKNOWLEDGMENTS

Writing a cookbook is a huge undertaking that requires the collaboration of many people, including food professionals, food-lovers, and friends and family. So, I'll take it from the top: to my publisher, Cameron + Co., and its amazing team—Chris Gruener, Pippa White, Iain Morris, Suzi Hutsell, and all the rest: Thank you for helping me to create this book. Chris, I like to work with people who lift me up, and I knew right away that you were one of those people. Pippa, thank you for helping me shape my ideas for *Homemade Simple*. Iain and Suzi, I could not have made it through this process without your hard work and determination.

To Kim Laidlaw, my editor: You're the best in the biz! You made every part of this book better.

To Kathleen Sheffer: Thank you for your great photographs that brought me and my food to life. And to Ann Murphy, whose photographs put the finishing touches on this enormous project!

To Caitlin Charlton, my cooking assistant: You are my right-hand woman and master of all things culinary.

To Lindsay Kinder: Thank you for your endless energy, creativity, and dedication to House of Haas, and for always encouraging me to go big in my business endeavors!

To my sons, Connor and Charlie: Charlie, you are my biggest critic, but that only helps make my work better. And Connor, you are the most grateful recipient of my cooking on earth. I love you boys so much.

To our second family, the Blisses: Sunny, Bill, Lindsey, Chase, and Brock: I couldn't have written this book without your requests, feedback, and appreciation for my cooking!

To my Earth angels: Karen Lott, Carolyn Luu, Amy Pierce, and Lindsay Kinder. You four were meant to be in my life for such special reasons. I cherish each of you so much.

To my biggest cheerleaders: Ellen Marie Bennett, Katie Couric, Ayesha Curry, Alisha Draney, Todd English, Tyler Florence, Tricia and Doro Bush Koch, Julie LaBarba, Kate Leahy, Jodi Liano, Shelley Lindgren, Jorge Mancheno, Diane Mina, Michael Mina, Kelley O'Brien, Tori Ritchie, James Schend, and Michelle Tam. Thank you for inspiring me and making me a better cook.

To Diablo Foods, including Connie, Daniel, and the entire team: Thank you for providing me with beautiful ingredients for the testing of these recipes. Your store continues to thrive because of the special people who work there!

To Madeline Feingold: Thank you for helping me envision and build a life for myself that I could treasure. I'm forever grateful to know you.

To my House of Haasers: Thanks to every one of you who signed up for the House of Haas. You supported my dream to write another cookbook and helped me test the recipes. I'm so grateful for the community we've created:

Katie Abraham, Janice Albert, Kimberly Allison, Liz Armstrong, Julie Baher, Maggie Barber, Craig Barnes, Kashe Barton, Carrie Baum, Carrie Beard, Denise Belt, Leighann Berg, Bernadette Betita, Sunny Bliss, Ellen Blommer, Allison Bouvier, Marianne Bowen, Clayton Boyer, Tracey Bracco, Myra Brent-McGarry, Anne Buffo, Lisa Burnham, Elizabeth Calder, Louise Caldwell, Jessica Canfield, Ingrid Carbone, Tammy Casatico, Diane Cassano, Donna M. Cecchi, Laura Cerda, Susan Christianson, Linda Citron, Kerry deGavre, Libby DeMeo, James Doherty, Susan Douglass, Alisha Draney, Nicole Dube, Laurie Duerksen, Dana DuFrane, Janet England, Loretta Esau, Courtney Fitzpatrick, Elizabeth Flaherty, Chris Flitter, Leslie French, Shannon Gainey, Alison Garraway, Carolyn Gatherers, Claudia Gohler, Michael Goldman, Shannon Gomes, Anne Goodnow, Chris Grimes, Dana Guerrero, Kathy Hare, Victoria Harrison, Jenny Hawkins, Nancy Hemry, Denise Henry, Rachel Hillis, Jeanie Hocking, Kim Holderness, Suzanne Hopkins, K.Q. Horton, DeAnn Huft, Kristen Hunt, Anne Hussey, Lucy Jackson, Lindsay Kinder, Dorothy Koch, Peggy Koltz, Lori Kretz, Tammy Kronen, Ruth Kuhn, Julie La Barba, Deanna La Croix, Elizabeth T. Lassiter, Mackenzie Lesher, Michelle Levine, Valerie Lewis, Janet Livingston, Janet Lowery, Ann Lyman, Christine MacConnell, Bernie Mahan, Linda Marrow, Heidi Maunder, Andee McKenzie, Jason McKinney, Patsy Mickens, Lori Mihaly,Fenna Millen, Diane Mina, Pamela Morgan, Erin Morris, Bina Motiram, Mary McKenna, Kim Noon, Kelley O'Brien, Sandra Osbaldeston, Karen Oshana, Marykay Park, Beverly Jane Peatross, Julie Pollard, Carol Potter, Helene Rayder, Meghan Read, Laura Revelos, Dana Rifat, Anne Ritchings, Cami Roberts, Barbara Robins, Darren Rose, Wendy Ross, Elaine Rusk, Alex Sacripante, Libby Schreiber, Sherry Segundo, Carol Seitz, Laurie Schultheiss Sellar, Kathleen Sheffer, Nancy Silver, Susan Silver, Gilda Simonian, Harley Smith, Amy Snook, Pamela Stafford, Susie Stagnaro, Stacey Stambleck, Helena Chevalier Stehlik, Allison Stokes, Pat Stone, Linda Linnerud Swensen, Katy Tafoya, Della Tall, Carrie Tan, Anne Marie Taylor, Susan Thomas, Erna Thompson, Laura Vida, Jeannie Vilary, Buzzy Waite, Deb Wallace, Lisa Waterman, Vanessa Webb, Erica Wehrs, Sandy K. Wells, Jean Willis-Brown, Julie Wright, and Cynthia Harbaugh.

INDEX

CAMERON + COMPANY
149 Kentucky Street, Suite 7
Petaluma, CA 94952
www.cameronbooks.com

PUBLISHER Chris Gruener
CREATIVE DIRECTOR Iain R. Morris
DESIGNER Emily Studer
MANAGING EDITOR Jan Hughes
EDITORIAL ASSISTANT Krista Keplinger

EXECUTIVE EDITOR Kim Laidlaw
PHOTOGRAPHERS Kathleen Sheffer
 and Ann Murphy
COPY EDITOR Carolyn Miller
PROOFREADER Amy Treadwell
INDEXER Ken Della Penta

Published in 2023 by CAMERON + COMPANY, an
imprint of ABRAMS. All rights reserved.

Library of Congress Cataloging-in-Publication
Data available.

ISBN: 978-1-949480-47-4

10 9 8 7 6 5 4 3 2

Printed in China